School Improvement

School Improvement

Let the Professional Standards for Educational Leaders Work for You

Edited by
Rocky Wallace
With Eve Proffitt and Stephanie Sullivan

ROWMAN & LITTLEFIELD
Lanham • Boulder • New York • London

Published by Rowman & Littlefield
An imprint of The Rowman & Littlefield Publishing Group, Inc.
4501 Forbes Boulevard, Suite 200, Lanham, Maryland 20706
www.rowman.com

6 Tinworth Street, London SE11 5AL, United Kingdom

British Library Cataloguing in Publication Information Available

Library of Congress Cataloging-in-Publication Data

Library of Congress Control Number: 2021933387

ISBN 978-1-4758-5990-4 (cloth : alk. paper)
ISBN 978-1-4758-5991-1 (pbk. : alk. paper)
ISBN 978-1-4758-5992-8 (electronic)

∞™ The paper used in this publication meets the minimum requirements of American National Standard for Information Sciences—Permanence of Paper for Printed Library Materials, ANSI/NISO Z39.48-1992.

Dedication

This book is dedicated to all of our education leadership partners in our neighboring colleges and universities across Kentucky, the Kentucky Department of Education's school leadership support team, our education cooperatives and other education leadership support agencies, and our school administrators in P-12 down in the trenches. The abundance of talented and caring school leaders we have across this state is such a blessing.

A special "thank you" to Dr. Eve Proffitt and Dr. Stephanie Sullivan, whose tireless giving of several days of their summer to contribute in major ways to the editing of this book made all the difference.

Rocky Wallace

Contents

Foreword

The exercise of leadership involves people: a leader or leaders, a follower or followers, and the interaction of their personalities, knowledge, skills, and moral predispositions.

—Stuart Smith and Philip Piele

Since the initial release of the Interstate School Leaders Licensure Consortium (ISLLC) *Standards for School Leaders* in 1996, educators, higher-ed faculty, and policy makers have been on a journey to understand the critical knowledge, skills, and dispositions that describe the complex exercise of school leadership. That standards-guided journey has evolved over more than two decades, and the latest milestone along the way is the wide adoption of the *Professional Standards for Educational Leaders* (PSEL, 2015).

Kentucky's Education Professional Standards Board adopted PSEL in December 2018 as the foundation for advanced educational leadership licensure across the Commonwealth. For the past two years, a diverse and committed group of Kentucky P12 and higher-education partners has been collaborating to articulate a coherent path forward to integrate PSEL from initial certification, to career entry, and on to a successful professional growth and development experience for school leaders throughout the course of their careers.

With support from the Wallace Foundation's University Principal Preparation Initiative (UPPI), our work group began to unpack and analyze PSEL standards to better understand what each standard and related elements look like in leadership preparation and actual practice. This book represents the best thinking and reflections of several members of our team, and we hope that readers find that it illuminates the PSEL as a way of thinking about the growth and effectiveness of educational leaders and how preparation programs, central offices, principal evaluators, and superintendents can provide timely and targeted supports and interventions for school leaders as they grow and improve.

One of my favorite parts of the PSEL is that each of the ten standards' statements ends with the phrase *each student's academic success and well-being.* Preparing school leaders to enter the profession grounded in these standards and focused on the academic success and well-being of each student is critically important work. School leadership matters—it matters to organizational culture, it matters to governance, it matters to communities, and, most importantly, it matters to student achievement. Kudos to these authors for their willingness to open the Kentucky process to review and for their service to the profession!

Lu S. Young, EdD
Associate Clinical Professor and Principal Program Faculty Chair
Department of Educational Leadership Studies
University of Kentucky College of Education

Introduction to Kentucky Professional Standards for Educational Leaders (PSEL)

Eve Proffitt

Strong public schools are crucial to ensuring equal opportunity for all Americans, an underpinning of our democracy. If headed by effective principals, schools stand a better chance of providing each and every student with the high-quality education essential for success in the 21st century.

—Wallace Foundation

In December 2018, the Kentucky Education Professional Standards Board (EPSB) adopted the Professional Standards for Educational Leaders (PSEL). The PSEL define the practice of an effective school leader as support for the academic success and well-being of each student. These standards guide administrator preparation, licensure, and evaluation in Kentucky. The PSEL are national professional standards as they communicate expectations to practitioners, supporting institutions, professional associations, policy makers, and the public about the work, qualities, and values of *effective* educational leaders. They are a compass guiding the direction of practice directly, via performance expectations of the profession as well as indirectly, by influencing the work of policy makers, professional associations, and supporting institutions.

Starting in 2018, stakeholders in Kentucky, including educator leader preparation faculty, principals, superintendents, diverse educational groups, and educational cooperative representatives, began the process of developing a rubric for PSEL by expanding the definition to include practices denoting exemplary, effective, developing, and ineffective principals. This work was an outgrowth of a collaborative process with universities and educational

1

cooperatives, which began in 2017 facilitated by the EPSB, called the *Kentucky University Principal Preparation Initiative*, as part of a Wallace Foundation grant.

As new educational leaders complete their preparation programs, lead their schools, and emerge as effective instructional leaders, it is imperative they keenly understand and respond to challenges, build supportive relationships with stakeholder communities, assess their district's equity context, and work within their building's unique culture to improve student success. As research substantiates, few candidates from preparation programs engage as new administrators in formal induction programs related to efficient and effective transition into their new roles. As preparation programs and school districts, it is important to focus on the specific skill set of principal candidates and new principals establishing a culture of support and coherence to guide them through their preparation experiences and the first critical year as new principals.

In response to this emergent need, the University Principal Preparation Initiative (UPPI) Wallace workgroup along with key stakeholders from school districts, regional cooperatives, universities, and education organizations collaborated, reviewed, and recommended to the EPSB board and to the Kentucky Department of Education (KDE) board adoption of the national PSEL. The EPSB board adopted the PSEL standards for all advanced administrative educator preparation programs in December 2018 and promulgated into *16 KAR 5:090*, effective July 1, 2019. The Kentucky Board of Education (KBE) adopted the PSEL standards upon recommendation from the Commissioner's Principal Advisory Committee (PrAC) in December 2019 and promulgated into *704 KAR 3:370*, effective July 2020.

Given the new regulations, the UPPI Wallace workgroup designed the "Kentucky Professional Standards for Educational Leaders Guidance for Growth and Evaluation." The virtual tool, anchored as an agent of growth and evaluation, provides support and guidance around determining a pathway for growth. In accordance with this vision, principals will have a network of support as they lead their schools to heightened achievement, understand how their work connects to that of the district, and develop the skills necessary to efficiently recognize and improve teacher *effectiveness*.

As a result, Kentucky principal preparation programs and school districts will focus on the standards aligned to improving instructional practice with specific, desired outcomes aimed at strengthening leadership capacity. The collaboration of preparation programs and school districts will enhance the development and growth of principals in the state.

School districts will guide principals through the development and implementation of a career plan, tailored to their individual leadership needs and deeply embedded in the Kentucky PSEL through four performance measures directly aligned to the Kentucky principal evaluation system. Per *704 KAR 3:370*, principal evaluations are to document performance in four areas: planning, environment, instruction, and professionalism.

On June 2, 2020, the Office of Educator Licensure and Effectiveness (OELE) released the PSEL Guidance for Growth and Evaluation Virtual Tool. This tool is designed to support principal mentors, preparation personnel, and supervisors in facilitating a growth process for principals. The goal of the PSEL guidance tool is to enhance professional practices of school leaders to *improve student outcomes*. It will serve our preparation programs as they design clinical and field experiences in partnership with district stakeholders for principal growth.

Expectations of current school leaders and conversations surrounding educational leadership are rapidly evolving. Today's principals must focus on instructional leadership, the cultivation of diversity in schools, the assurance of equal access to equitable opportunities leading to the highest levels of learning and achievement for all students, and ensuring safe schools. The PSEL are intended to inform the work of preparation programs and school leaders and impact leadership development over the next decade.

In addition to developing the PSEL Guidance for Growth and Evaluation Virtual Tool, Kentucky also developed a PSEL Professional Learning Series. This series consists of six modules, which are described more in chapter 11. They are one of the support systems in place in Kentucky for aspiring leader candidates and school leaders.

The following chapters are descriptors of the PSEL in Kentucky, including expectations, outcomes, and case stories. Each of the PSEL constitutes a chapter, 1–10. Chapter 11 addresses how Kentucky is implementing the standards. Chapter 12 provides additional insight into an example of leadership. It is anticipated this book will not only support principal candidates but also school leaders as they continue to grow in leading Kentucky schools.

Chapter 1

Mission, Vision, and Core Values

James G. Allen and Ginger R. Blackwell

You've got to think about the big things while you're doing small things so that all of the small things go in the right direction.

—Alvin Toffler, Futurist

Standard 1: Effective educational leaders develop, advocate, and enact a shared mission, vision, and core values of high-quality education and academic success and well-being of each student.

a) *Develop an educational mission for the school to promote the academic success and well-being of each student.*

Mission is often defined as the fundamental purpose of existence. So why do schools exist? More importantly, why does YOUR school exist? Great principals know that schools are only successful when everyone in the building shares a *student-centered* purpose, and they take steps to make that happen. While academic achievement remains a top priority, today's principals must also view the social and emotional well-being of students in their care as equally significant.

To develop an educational mission for your school is to create a roadmap with signposts along the path promoting the academic success and well-being of each student. Each of these signposts—the goals and activities in your school—must be aligned with a strategic directional plan pointing toward the ultimate destination. There should be no detours or U-turns, as these should be avoided. The vision, then, is the ultimate destination.

b) *In collaboration with members of the school and the community and using relevant data, develop and promote a vision for the school on the successful learning and development of each child and on instructional and organizational practices that promote such success.*

Great principals must know a lot about a lot of things. They are good managers and knowledgeable instructional coaches. Most of all, they know the importance of recognizing their students as individuals. Data are analyzed to inform instruction, and instructional practices are tailored to meet the needs of the students and move each one forward.

Even though the principal plays a crucial role, there is simply no way one individual can do everything that needs to be done in a school. Effective principals ensure that they bring others along by including representatives from the various roles that make up the school community in the process of developing a shared vision for what they want the school to look like if they are truly living their student-centered mission. Together, they determine what the final destination should look like and how they will know when they have arrived. An effective vision is clearly stated and allows each stakeholder to see his or her role in that vision. It then becomes the basis for which all decisions in the school are made.

c) *Articulate, advocate, and cultivate core values that define the school's culture and stress the imperative of child-centered education; high expectations and student support; equity, inclusiveness, and social justice; openness, caring, and trust; and continuous improvement.*

Schools exist to educate children, and students cannot learn if they do not feel safe and welcome. Therefore, the core values of your school should be centered around creating an environment that is safe and welcoming for ALL students. Creating and maintaining a student-centered environment can be harder than it sounds. Competing interests and a desire to please everyone can lead some principals to struggle with this; therefore, the best principals keep a laser-like focus on what is best for the students. They model fairness and acceptance of their diverse student populations; in fact, they celebrate this diversity and strive to create an equitable environment for all. They implement and support instructional practices, such as providing time for true professional learning communities, which lead to continuous improvement for each child.

d) *Strategically develop, implement, and evaluate actions to achieve the vision for the school.*

How will you know if your school is truly living up to its mission and vision? Effective principals know that measurable objectives need to be put in place and frequently monitored. These "pulse checks" help ensure the school stays on the right path and progress is being made toward that vision. Again, the vision—one that has been collaboratively developed and agreed upon by all stakeholders, should be implemented and evaluated as the basis for all decisions within the school.

e) *Review the school's mission and vision and adjust them to changing expectations and opportunities for the school and changing needs and situations of students.*

How many members of your faculty and staff can articulate the school's mission, vision, and core values? Are these simply words that are hanging in the school's office or posted somewhere on the website? If so, they are meaningless.

Effective school leaders do not become complacent once the vision and mission have been created for their school. They know that these need to be living, breathing documents if they are to bring actual change to the school. This means that school leaders frequently talk about what the school would look like if everyone is truly living the mission. For example, in reference to the vision, or final destination, what kinds of things will they see when they arrive? What will they hear? How will people treat one another and hold one another accountable in this final destination?

Every major decision made is looked at from the perspective of how it will help move the school closer to its ideal vision. Great leaders recognize that schools change. Student populations change. State requirements change. New faculty are brought on board. Therefore, it is crucial that the school's mission, vision, and core values are reviewed and revised frequently so that everyone stays on the same pathway. Included should be short- and long-term goals and activities that can be adjusted throughout the school year as the school encounters detours, rest stops, and roadblocks. Using the mission and vision in this way provides clarity of purpose and keeps all of your arrows appropriately lined up toward the ending destination.

f) *Develop a shared understanding of and commitment to mission, vision, and core values within the school and the community.*

Developing a shared understanding stems from being an excellent communicator; being able to build consensus around the vision, mission, and core values; and being deliberate about involving stakeholders from the beginning of the process and throughout the journey.

Once the mission, vision, and core values have been developed, an excellent school leader knows that he or she must communicate often using a variety of modes of communication. There is no such thing as overcommunication when it comes to getting the school's vision out there. Opening day meetings provide opportune times to share the school's vision with all faculty and staff. It is a good reminder for those returning and crucial for all new hires.

The mission and vision should be prominently displayed in the building and on the school website. Most importantly, school leaders should explicitly make connections between all office's decisions and the mission, vision, and core values upon which the school has agreed.

g) *Model and pursue the school's mission, vision, and core values in all aspects of leadership.*

When assuming a leadership position in a school, someone is always watching to see if the leader's actions match his or her words. As a result, effective leaders know that they must model the school's mission, vision, and core values every day in every way. Teachers want to know that even if the principal makes decisions they do not agree with, they can still know that the principal is doing what he or she believes is best for students. Both teachers and students alike want to feel safe, welcome, and respected. In short, leaders have to talk the talk and walk the walk.

SCENARIO

Conflicting Interests

It was that time of year again—May. After three years as principal of the middle school, which she herself had attended as an adolescent, Dawn had been dreading sending out the master schedule to all of the teachers. Reluctantly, she attached the schedule that read "DRAFT" in large letters across the middle, thought a second, and then hit send on her email. She knew she was in for a long night.

Dawn had been a model student in her seventh grade science teacher's class. In fact, Ms. Thomas was a large part of the reason Dawn had decided to pursue education as a career herself. She loved her class and wanted to inspire her students, just as Ms. Thomas had inspired her. Years later, Ms. Thomas had even been a member of the School Based Decision Making (SBDM) Council who selected Dawn as the school's next principal. In her interview, Dawn shared that it would be her goal to make every decision based on the best interests of the students. The hiring committee agreed with this sentiment and recommended her for the job. Dawn could not have been happier.

In fact, Dawn had always considered herself to be a very student-centered educator. One of the first things she did when she started in her new role as principal was to facilitate a group of stakeholders in the development of a new mission and vision, and core values. Everyone was very proud of this effort and agreed that all decisions should be made in alignment with these agreed-upon goals.

Now, three years later, Dawn was recognizing that this was easier said than done. Due to increased enrollment for the upcoming year, Ms. Thomas, who had only taught seventh grade science for twenty-five years, would now be asked to teach a section of eighth grade science. Dawn knew that Ms. Thomas would not be happy with this decision, and she was not looking forward to the inevitable discussion that she knew was coming. She shut down her computer, went home for a late dinner and experienced a restless night of sleep.

At 7 a.m. the next morning, Dawn grabbed her coffee and sat down at her desk. As she turned toward her computer to turn it back on, she heard a knock at her door. She turned around to see a very angry Ms. Thomas demanding a word with her.

What is an appropriate response? How would you handle this situation?

Mission-Focused Leaders:

- have excellent communication skills and are easily understood.
- listen.
- know their schools (students, teachers, and community) well.

- are collaborative and bring people together.
- are inclusive and model respect for all people.
- make all decisions based on what is best for students.
- inspire enthusiasm and commitment.
- are intentional and strategic.
- are consensus builders.
- are flexible, responsive, and proactive.
- create an environment that is safe and welcoming for all.
- make data-driven decisions.
- remain student-centered rather that adult centered.
- model the school's mission, vision, and core values in all areas of personal and professional life.
- reference the school's mission, vision, and core values in the decision-making process.

Questions for Further Reflection:

1. Examine your school's vision statement (or another one with which you are familiar). What is your assessment of this statement? How is the vision communicated with members of the school community? In what ways do you (or your school leaders) articulate and steward the school's vision? What could be changed or improved?
2. After reflecting on the above scenario, *Conflicting Interests*, what would you do in this situation? If Dawn could go back in time, what are some things she could do differently in order to change the outcome?
3. As a school administrator, one is bombarded with conflicting priorities and interests on a daily basis. Without an intentional focus, one can easily become scattered and unfocused. Think about the best school administrators you know. What specific steps do these leaders take in order to keep the focus on their school's mission, vision, and core values?
4. What is the relationship between a school's mission, vision, and core values and those of the district?

Chapter 2

Ethical and Professional Norms

Rocky Wallace and Franklin Thomas

The best leaders are clear. They continually light the way, and in the process, let each person know that what they do makes a difference. The best test as a leader is: Do those served grow as persons; do they become healthier, wiser, freer, more autonomous, more likely themselves to become leaders?

—Robert K. Greenleaf

Standard 2: Effective educational leaders act ethically and according to professional norms to promote each student's academic success and well-being.

a) *Act ethically and professionally in personal conduct, relationships with others, decision-making, stewardship of the school's resources, and all aspects of school leadership.*

So, the expectation is for the school leader to be a role model for the entire community? Well, yes. This assumption has always been the case, but more so now than ever before. Gone are the days of "work is work, and home is home," and my private life is my business. With the advent of the internet and the array of social media access that goes with it, the school leader, and all public officials, are easy prey for those who wish to post anything—whether opinion, picture(s), video(s)—about anybody.

If the school superintendent or principal, for example, is not living up to the standards of serving the community at large as a positive role model, then somewhere down the line the reality and the expectations will collide, and the school and/or district will be hurt, not to mention the school leader and his/her family.

And of course, modeling healthy relationships at school and in the community, putting students first with ethical decision-making on their behalf, and being an effective *gatekeeper* of the school—including its various human, physical, and fiscal resources—are all vital attributes that are expected from the school leader of the twenty-first century. Simply put, if one is not comfortable with these expectations, it's best to not jump into the arena at this level.

b) *Act according to and promote the professional norms of integrity, fairness, transparency, trust, collaboration, perseverance, learning, and continuous improvement.*

In working with hundreds, maybe thousands, of school leaders over the years, never do they describe themselves as having low integrity. You'll be no exception to that rule, correct? Are you sure? You won't truly know until you are tested and pass the test. You may find yourself securing the money from the ticket sales to a big rivalry basketball game and realize that you can take a little of that money, *doctor* the paperwork, and no one will notice. It is at that moment that your integrity will be tested, and of course, you need to pass that test. You need to welcome the opportunity to pass those tests from time to time.

And then there is *fairness*. Am I a "fair" person? It is difficult to have a succinct definition for the word fair. There is tension between the egalitarian theory, which says that everyone should be treated the same, and the utilitarian theory, which says that fairness is what produces the most benefit as a whole. Philosophers have tried for centuries to define fairness, so good luck.

Transparency is, perhaps, easier to define. But let's start by defining what it is not. It does not mean translucent. Translucent means that the light passing through to our eyes may be bent a bit. So, if we are mostly transparent in our practice as administrators, but occasionally bend information a bit, then we are translucent rather than transparent. Have you ever heard a leader say that they pride themselves in their translucency? You probably have not. It just doesn't have a good ring to it. But this concept is all or nothing. You're either transparent and can be proud of it, or you're not and probably just don't need to bring it up.

School leaders should strive to be transparent because that will take them halfway to earning the next concept, which is "trust." The remaining journey to becoming trustworthy involves making sure that leaders follow through with their promises. So, be careful what you promise!

Collaboration is one of those "soft skills" that we hear so much about these days. These skills are now considered so important that job applicants sometimes have to pass a test about them before they can be considered. So, that means that leaders need to develop skills in collaboration! In order to accomplish that, a school leader must learn to listen and compromise.

That doesn't sound too difficult, but here's the rub. School leaders must promote collaboration among those they supervise. It gets worse. A school leader is not truly promoting collaboration if the matter is mandated. "I order you all to collaborate!" No, it is the school leaders responsibility to create a collaborative environment.

Perseverance is a trait that will serve school leaders well. When the job gets tough, a leader cannot give up. The goal that has been set must be achieved, regardless of the obstacles. A leader must be all in. When confronting failures, the effective leader must pick himself up, dust himself off, and adapt. It may take baby steps, but with perseverance the goal can be reached. As the old saying goes. There's only one way to eat an elephant: one bite at a time.

The concept of *continual improvement* can be illustrated to people by them to "always keep the bow of the boat pointed upward." If you follow this rule and always strive to be at least just a little better, then you have continual improvement. Learning is key to being able to achieve this.

Once a leader has earned a terminal degree, the box regarding learning can be checked, correct? Not even close. Think of learning as lifelong learning. Educators who began teaching thirty years ago didn't even have computers in the classroom. Now those same educators may be teaching exclusively using a computer to reach students all around the nation. That took some learning! And, the learning does not stop there. What will that educator need to learn next to continually meet the academic needs of students?

c) *Place children at the center of education and accept responsibility for each student's academic success and well-being.*

"Place children at the center of education?" Of course! Who else would we place at the center of education? The adults. That's who. A leader must answer the following question with brutal honesty. Do we make decisions based upon what benefits students, or do we make decisions based upon what benefits adults and makes their lives easier? This is another all or nothing situation. Are we student-centered all of the time? If not, then don't think about writing a mission statement claiming that your school is student-centered.

And then there's that pesky word *each* that makes a leader's job so much more challenging and rewarding than if the word was *some*. We have to accept responsibility for *each* student. That means the student with a disability AND the gifted student, the kid whose father is a rich doctor AND the migrant child who speaks limited English, the captain of the basketball team AND the awkward kid who gets bullied.

And there's one more challenge. We have to be concerned with students' "academic success and well-being." Educators understand the former, but exactly what is *well-being*? It's no big deal, really. It just means that we have to ensure that students are healthy and happy.

d) *Safeguard and promote the values of democracy, individual freedom and responsibility, equity, social justice, community, and diversity.*

"Safeguard and promote the values of democracy." This statement is then followed by several other concepts that actually do a fine job of describing the values of democracy, except patriotism may need to be added to the list.

First in the list is individual freedom and responsibility. Adults and students need to realize two things about freedom in schools and in the world in general. First, freedom is a wonderful thing. Just ask someone who has never experienced freedom or lost that privilege for a period of time. Second, and in contrast, freedom must have limits, or you have something called anarchy. The ideal degree of "limits" on freedom in schools and in the world, in general, is a delicate balance.

The next concept of *individual responsibility* is a trait that is on life support in our society. This concept can mean that an individual takes responsibility for oneself, but more commonly means an individual takes responsibility for his actions. When teachers are given the glamorous assignment of checking the restrooms, occasionally a student may be found holding a lit cigarette. Often students quickly throw the evidence into the toilet. Students often fail to take responsibility for their actions and deny that they were smoking, or they may claim that they had been holding the cigarette for another student, for whom they conveniently cannot recall the name.

The concept of "equity" really needs to be discussed with the next concept of "social justice" and also with another term equality. Consider School A that is located in a historically poor neighborhood. Also consider School B in the same school district that is located in a historically affluent neighborhood. School B gets donations from wealthy alumni and from businesses within the community. School A does not. The district would be practicing equality if it funded both schools at an "equal" per student amount. The district would be practicing equity if it gave additional funding to School A to offset the lack of outside funding sources.

To rephrase a popular quote, it could be said, "There is nothing less equitable than the equal treatment of unequals." In the above example, the district would be practicing social justice if it joined initiatives to improve the prosperity of the neighborhood around School A to remove the barriers that the school was experiencing.

Promoting the concept of "community" among students helps the students by providing them a sense of belonging. It is also important to encourage students to contribute to their community in some manner. Don't forget to stretch the definition of "community." This term doesn't just refer to location but also to other manifestations such as students' identities and organizations. These extensions of the concept of community have become more pronounced as electronic communication has proliferated.

There are many sources of *diversity* in schools, including culture, race, religion, gender, sexual orientation, and disabilities. Diversity can present many challenges. For example, if your school includes a large number of students whose primary language is not English, communication and teaching these students will be a challenge. At the same time, diversity can present many opportunities. For example, if your school includes a large number of students from different cultures, they can teach their classmates about other cultures much better than a book. Administrators should always keep in mind that diversity issues can sometimes be very controversial.

e) *Lead with interpersonal and communication skill, social-emotional insight, and understanding of all students' and staff members' backgrounds and cultures.*

So often leaders think of "interpersonal and communication skill" as the effective flow of information from themselves to others using concepts such as clarity, brevity, giving feedback, developing trust, and having empathy. While this is important, managing inflowing information is just as important. This entails skills such as careful listening, attention to nonverbal clues, and asking questions. *Social-emotional insight* includes many of these same skills and a few others, such as developing positive relationships, managing emotions, and having empathy. Empathy merits a second mention because it is such an important concept.

Leaders need to have an understanding of all students' and staff members' backgrounds and cultures. *Understanding a person's background* means understanding things such as where they are from, their family and personal history, their level of affluence, religious preference, and their linguistic skills. Leaders are supposed to know all of that about all students and staff members? If so, you will need to have lots of effective communication with lots of people and you'll need to have an outstanding memory.

For administrators who do not trust their memory, yet know the importance of having knowledge about their employees, it may be helpful to have memory aids to assist with recollection. One district administrator had a little packet of note cards, one for each employee, for each school.

f) *Provide moral direction for the school and promote ethical and professional behavior among faculty and staff.*

An administrator must provide moral direction for the school. *Moral direction* is a lofty concept and the administrator must provide this for the entire school? Nobody said that this job was going to be easy. This won't seem like such a daunting task if you simply set an example by following your school's student code of conduct and/or exemplify the school's statement of values. These statements of values often include behaviors such as good manners, sharing, and helping.

When you're accomplished at being the moral compass for your school, then you'll also need to "promote ethical and professional behavior among faculty and staff." These individuals may occasionally require a bit of corrective action, but a starting point and most of the battle is, once again, being a good role model. You must model integrity, transparency, and fairness. You must show up for work promptly and *dressed for the part* of being a role model. You must be organized and ready to follow through on what you say.

You must exude competence, not conceit, and a work ethic. You have to set your mind to always remaining poised under fire.

SCENARIO

Bill could not contain his excitement as he burst into the door: "Honey, guess what?"

And Melissa could not pretend she was oblivious to what he was going to say: "You got the job!"

"How did you know? I did!"

"I just had a feeling, when you were called back for a second interview. I am so proud of you, Bill! When do you begin?"

"Actually, this Monday. So, I better get plenty of sleep this weekend. Come on, I'm taking you out for a Friday night dinner and a movie."

Bill could not concentrate on the movie, as he kept thinking, "I am a school principal. Oh my, how will I get everything done before school starts in a couple of weeks?" He was happy, excited, nervous, doubtful of his abilities and also in awe of the opportunity all at the same time.

Monday morning came fast, and as he kissed the kids goodbye after breakfast, Bill thought to himself, "This is the last time I'll ever feel exactly this way as I head off to school."

And, oh my, as he worked through the pile of summer mail, post-it notes left by his secretary, phone calls from the district office, and began mapping out the countdown to opening day with his new assistant principal, Mrs. Johnson, Bill realized that what he had been told in his Master's program was indeed true: "Never a dull moment—something different to work on or take care of every five minutes." But, he loved it. He absolutely loved it.

The two weeks leading up to the beginning of fall semester went by like a blur, and Bill found himself being bombarded with all kinds of questions from staff and parents about what seemed like an endless list of decisions he apparently was supposed to make before school began. He sat down with Mrs. Johnson on the eve of opening day and asked her to make a list as he processed.

"We're both new to this. We'll have to work smart and help the staff develop a set of core values. You know, non-negotiables. I haven't seen anything posted or in writing about what they are. Often, they're assumed. But that's not good enough for us right now. You and I will be eaten alive if we don't help this staff chart a path that has a bold vision and impeccable ethics."

Mrs. Johnson smiled in agreement, and jotted down all kinds of good ideas as she and Bill took turns articulating what needed to be addressed, what priorities came first, how to develop a leadership team, how to celebrate successes from Day 1 and how to grow a culture of care and effectiveness.

And then came the first real test. Opening day flowed smoothly without a hitch, and everyone was excited to meet their new administrators. The buses were coming back in from their PM routes, and Bill was turning off the lights to his office, when he was interrupted by unannounced visitors.

"Hello Bill. May we speak to you for a moment?"

"Sure, walk me to my car."

No, this is going to take a while. You see, we're the three men who have basically run the basketball program for this school for the past several years. And frankly, the last principal didn't care one way or the other about the sports offered here. As a result, we have the weakest elementary team in the area. It's embarrassing. We thought with you being new and all, we'd bring you up to speed and share with you what this school needs if we're going to continue to pretend to grow basketball players here.

Bill politely invited the men in and sat down with them at the conference table in his office. He grabbed a pad and pen from his desk and simply took notes as the three voiced frustrations that spilled over into more than simply athletics. The venting went on for about 20 minutes, and Bill simply nodded and wrote until the air was cleared and the room was quiet.

Fellas, wow, you've shared a lot of concerns with me here today, and I appreciate it. As you might imagine, I have lots of other folks to meet with and various work teams to put in place. I already have on my calendar to meet one evening next week with the athletic boosters and any other parents who want to attend. You've given me a head start on what we'll need to better organize. Surely with all of the parents who want this school to succeed, we can come up with a plan that builds a top of the line sports program here. And, I want intramurals to be a part of the mix . . . . Friday evenings and Saturdays, and we need more than one sport too . . . . Lots of kids here have never worn a uniform before, never even had the opportunity to be on a team. That's gotta change.

"But what about the varsity teams? What about your athletes that will have a chance to go on to play high school ball, maybe college?"

"Oh, we'll provide a quality opportunity for them too—maybe traveling squads in addition to intramurals. Remember, this is elementary. So, the role we play is providing a broad range of opportunities for all of the kids. I'm sure after we've had input from other parents, we'll come up with something that is better than ever. Will you guys help us with this?"

The man who had done most of the talking nodded his head yes. "But what about these other issues? Gosh, there's so many. This school is falling apart."

Bill looked intently into his eyes, tempted to retort in an aggressive tone—but instead smiled.

Well, I'm meeting with groups of folks every day these next two weeks, just like I am here with you guys. We're making sure our curriculum is what it needs to be top to bottom, working on the schedule of PTA activities for this year, bringing three new teachers on board—including our first full-time music teacher, tweaking our master schedule so we can have an early morning school-wide reading block, rolling out a new math program for our primary grades ... I wouldn't exactly say this school is falling apart. The previous principal did a lot of great work here, and it shows. She set the table, and if all of us work together, the sky's the limit.

"I had tentatively planned for the athletic boosters meeting to be next Thursday evening, say 6 PM? No longer than an hour, tops. Sure would like you guys to be there. We'll need your support and experience."

Bill walked in the front door thirty minutes later than he had planned, and his family was sitting patiently—waiting on him for supper. Melissa looked at him and smiled with a puckered lip.

"Rough first day, Honey?"

"Sorry I'm late gang. I guess this may be the new normal some evenings." And then he looked out the window and talked to himself and his family all at the same time.

"No, it was a good day. A real good day . . . . Especially at the end. I met with the cabal."

Melissa looked surprised. "Cabal?"

"Yea. Nice guys . . . . You know what? I can do this—gonna be an adventure for sure."

Ethical School Leaders:

- are present, modeling the core value of being there.
- bring people together.
- keep the focus on what's best for students.
- are visible around the building.
- find time for short chats with staff.
- have a meal in the lunchroom with students from time to time.
- model strong emotional intelligence, and listen respectfully to parents, staff, students, and other stakeholders when they need to vent or share ideas.
- follow school and district fiscal and other policy protocol.
- help develop new policy when needed.
- empower and develop work teams.
- mentor and coach all staff and volunteers effectively.
- support and advocate for all students served by special services, and their families.
- support and advocate for ongoing professional development for staff.
- support and advocate for high-quality and age-appropriate curriculum.
- support and advocate for the arts.
- support and advocate for other enrichment opportunities that are not part of the core curriculum.
- support and advocate for best practice instruction in every classroom.
- support and advocate for cultural diversity, guest speakers, field trips, career days, health and science fairs (as well as other disciplines), talent shows, and other opportunities for students to experience a rich co-curriculum.
- support and advocate for sports and other extracurricular activities.
- support and advocate for student clubs.
- support and advocate for student opportunities as they prepare to leave his/her school or go on to post-secondary.
- hire the best applicants for posted positions.
- develop a positive relationship with the district office.
- develop supportive partnerships with other education agencies.
- develop supportive partnerships with community stakeholders.
- model an attitude of celebration of student and staff successes.
- model strong character and core values that set the tone for the school and community.

- handle conflict with respect and an open mind for all parties involved.
- model honorable speech.
- model love and support of family.

The ethical leader serves with authentic care for others, and without pretense. "Doing the right thing, at the right time, for the right reason" is the litmus test. No, not easy. But for sure, walking this "road less traveled" has priceless impact and influence on the present, and the future.

Questions for Further Reflection:

1. What areas of school leadership present the most challenge to you in fulfilling the moral commitment and obligation to serve as a caring, ethical role model and leader?
2. What past mentors have had a helpful influence on you in growing into this leadership position?
3. What suggestions would you have for aspiring school leaders?

Chapter 3

Equity and Cultural Responsiveness

Janet L. Applin

A school or district leader cannot help others address their biases until she is able to recognize and talk about her own.

—Irma Zardoya

Standard 3: Effective educational leaders strive for equity of educational opportunity and culturally responsive practices to promote each student's academic success and well-being.

a) *Ensure that each student is treated fairly, respectfully, and with an understanding of each student's culture and context.*

It sounds so simple, yet to ensure that each student is treated fairly, respectfully, and with an understanding of his or her culture and context is asking a lot of the school leader in one short sentence. A school leader must treat each student fairly. A school leader must treat students respectfully. A school leader does so while understanding each student's culture and context. All would agree that this is best practice for a school leader.

Yet, the opposite does happen, and the unfairness, disrespect, and lack of understanding of a student's culture and context can be so systemic in some places, people no longer notice. In addition, some families may be marginalized and treated unfairly, disrespectfully, and with little understanding of their culture or context. They may not feel comfortable speaking out or calling out a school leader.

School leaders need to recognize and acknowledge their own biases before they can ensure that each student is treated fairly, respectfully, and with an understanding of each student's culture and context. These biases must be acknowledged and overcome to prevent creating a system of inequity. As a leader, you must be prepared to create a culture that addresses each of these such that each student can be successful.

b) *Recognize, respect, and employ each student's strengths, diversity, and culture as assets for teaching and learning.*

It's easy for school leaders to recognize those outstanding students who seem to excel at everything—academics, athletics, and social skills. Those are the exceptions and the minority of students in a school or district. It's the other students who often go unnoticed in the limelight of those shining stars.

Does every child really have strengths? Do you really believe this? Can you model for those you lead how to recognize, respect, and employ those strengths, diversity, and culture as assets for teaching and learning? The answer is YES, and YOU MUST. Sometimes you really have to dig to find those strengths, but every child has them.

What do we mean when we talk about "diversity" in the schools? We are talking about individuals with diverse cultures, language, exceptionalities, and socioeconomic diversities. Maybe you think because you don't live in a large urban area that this standard doesn't apply to you. Even in small, rural schools where everyone appears to look alike, there are many, many diverse backgrounds and experiences present. It is your job to recognize and acknowledge those diverse students and teachers, find their strengths, and employ those strengths as an asset for teaching and learning.

c) *Ensure that each student has equitable access to effective teachers, learning opportunities, academic and social support, and other resources necessary for success.*

Wow, this sub-domain encompasses everything that you will do as a school leader! Your job is to make sure that every student has EQUITABLE access to effective teachers, opportunities, AND social support. Yep—this one includes the kitchen sink! You have to make sure you are thinking about this sub-domain when you are interviewing, hiring, and evaluating all of your staff. Next you must make sure that those staff have the resources they need to engage students with best practices—academically and emotionally—AND you must make sure that every child has this outstanding teacher. Whew! Have the people who wrote these standards ever tried to fill a high need teaching position two weeks before school starts?

This is what you signed up for when you chose to become a school leader, and the buck truly does stop with you. Does that mean that it is always attainable? Probably not, but it should be in the forefront of what you are looking for when you are staffing your school and district, allocating budget items for instruction and support services, and allocating those services throughout your school and district.

d) *Develop student policies and address student misconduct in a positive, fair, and unbiased manner.*

It is well documented that students of color and students with disabilities are disproportionately impacted by in-school and out-of-school suspensions and expulsions. In fact, according to the Civil Rights Data Collection, black students are suspended and expelled at a rate three times greater than white students, while students with disabilities are twice as likely to receive an out-of-school suspension as their nondisabled peers.

What should effective school leaders do to ensure their policies are not adding to common inequities in the system? We know that removing students from instruction through suspensions and expulsions is not the answer. There are well-researched alternatives to suspension such as school-wide positive behavior interventions, and these interventions have been shown to improve and reinforce positive, productive behaviors and also to increase academic engagement and achievement. Wow, improved behavior AND increased academic achievement? It's two for the price of one. Why would you do anything else? School leaders must be well versed on and utilize these evidence-based tools at their disposal to assist in developing policies that are positive, fair and unbiased for all students under their charge.

e) *Confront and alter institutional biases of student marginalization, deficit-based schooling, and low expectations associated with race, class, culture and language, gender and sexual orientation, and disability or special status.*

Have you ever seen someone roll their eyes and shrug their shoulders when a child fails or drops out of school? It's that, "What are ya gonna do?" attitude that has allowed too many children to experience the self-fulfilling prophesies of low expectations. Educational leaders MUST not allow this attitude to go unnoticed or unaddressed. Educational leaders must model a zero tolerance for institutional biases of student marginalization, deficit-based schooling, and low expectations associated with diversity.

Confronting biases and student marginalization may not make you popular to those who have upheld the status-quo, but you may be surprised to find out how many people were secretly cheering for you when you finally let it be known that this behavior is no longer acceptable with you as the educational leader at the helm.

f) *Promote the preparation of students to live productively in and contribute to the diverse cultural contexts of a global society.*

Preparing students only to be proficient in the traditional core content subjects like reading, writing, math, science, social studies, and even the arts is not going to prepare them to live productively and contribute to the diverse cultural contexts of a global society. That may have been good enough half a century ago, but it is no longer considered what is needed for success in college, career, and citizenship in the twenty-first century. The National Education Association and other education leaders believe that students must be proficient in the "Four Cs" to compete in a global society: Critical Thinking and Problem Solving, Communication, Collaboration, and Creativity and Innovation.

Your job as an educational leader is to promote the preparation of students to be proficient in their academic preparation as well as the Four Cs to contribute to the diverse cultural contexts of a global society. You must ensure that those whom you lead are ready to take on the challenge of preparing students for a global society—even if it may be from a small, rural, school district.

g) *Act with cultural competence and responsiveness in their interactions, decision-making, and practice.*

Most of us, if asked if we know what it means to be culturally competent and responsive in our practices would answer, "Yes!" But what if you were asked to describe what that looks like in a school leader? Could you answer it as quickly? In a review of culturally responsive school leadership, Khalifa, Gooden, and Davis[1] provide four behavioral strands seen in culturally responsive school leaders: Critical Self-Awareness; Culturally Responsive Curricula and Teacher Preparation; Culturally Responsive and Inclusive School Environments; and Engaging Students and Parents in Community Contexts.

Culturally Responsive School Leadership is an emerging field, and Khalifa's, *et al.*,[2] strands are admittedly not exhaustive, but they are a starting framework to find one's own way of interacting, decision-making, and practicing cultural responsiveness.

h) *Address matters of equity and cultural responsiveness in all aspects of leadership.*

This element is really the catch-all for all of the other areas of this standard. If it is not addressed in the other sub-elements, it is made up for here. Educational leaders must address matters of equity and cultural responsiveness in ALL ASPECTS OF LEADERSHIP. Yes, that's right—everything you do as an educational leader should be grounded with thoughts of equity and cultural responsiveness.

As you make decisions on your mission, vision and core values, equity and cultural responsiveness should be part of those core values. As you grapple with ethics and moral dilemmas, equity and cultural responsiveness should be part of your ethical decision-making process. As you develop and support curriculum, instruction, and assessment, you must consider equity and cultural responsiveness.

As you strive to cultivate a community of care and support for students, you've got it, you must cultivate that community with an awareness of equity and cultural responsiveness. The sub-element requires that you are constantly thinking about matters of equity and cultural responsiveness. It is to be embedded in every task you complete, every decision you ponder, every staff member you hire, every interaction you have with a student and his or her family—yes, every single part of your job as an educational leader.

"Because minoritized students have been disadvantaged by historically oppressive structures, and because educators and schools have been— intentionally or unintentionally—complicit in reproducing this oppression,

culturally responsive school leaders have a principled, moral responsibility to counter this oppression."[3]

Culturally Responsive Leaders:

- model respect for students, parents, staff, and community members from all backgrounds.
- develop authentic and trusting relationships with all stakeholders.
- are proactive in addressing a toxic culture of bias and privileged thinking.
- seek out a diverse mix of staff and volunteers to meet the ethnic needs of the school community.
- model an appreciation for the uniqueness of the local school's community culture.
- are proactive in addressing harassment of any kind.
- are culturally sensitive to the various ethnic groups in the school population.
- are aware of bullying or taunting issues, and proactive in confronting the perpetrators.
- create a "voice of reason" within the school and community in improving ethnic relations.
- provide training for all staff in the understanding of deliberate or incidental bias.
- provide opportunities for all students to be involved in co-curricular and extracurricular clubs and activities that meet the diverse needs of the student population.
- facilitate the creation of school and district policies that address ethnic, social and academic bias.
- create an atmosphere of openness and education for all stakeholders in the areas of bias and "tribal" exclusion.
- coordinate a comprehensive menu of student services and opportunities that is rich in the arts, and embraces learning more about local, regional, national, and international cultures and customs.

SCENARIO

Martin was dreading going to school on this day, as the annual talent showcase was taking place in the high school gym for most of the morning. He had somehow not noticed the invitation for students to submit a proposal to perform or display their unique abilities/creations on stage in front of the student body. He begged his mom to let him stay home, but she would not allow it.

"Mom, it's just the same ol' stuff. A few students every year get up and strut around playing guitar, doing dances, singing, and telling a few jokes. It's not really for all of us—mainly just the popular kids."

Martin's mother stopped doing the breakfast dishes and stared at him with surprise and an air of disgust. "So, you've never been asked to showcase your art? Or it's never been acknowledged at school that you've already written three published children's books?"

"Mom, no. Why would I go around bragging about stuff like that?"

"Martin, why would you not? It's a real big deal. I thought you were in the writer's club?"

"It disbanded this past fall . . . . We just had four of us in it, so the faculty sponsor didn't have time."

"What about the art club?"

"It meets after school at the same time our yearbook club meets, so I had to choose."

"Did you miss the invite to take part in the talent show?"

"I guess so. My buddy Charlie told me it came around about a month ago in an e-mail."

"That's it? One e-mail?"

"Pretty much."

"Martin, you know how your father and I feel about these things. Our parents were immigrants. He has Italian roots and I have Hispanic roots. You speak three languages—fluently. We would never ask you to flaunt your talents or be prideful. But this goes deeper than that. We do expect you to advocate for diversity, and for the due recognition and acceptance that you and all of your classmates deserve."

"Mom-m-m, it's not an issue with me. I know I'm a gifted writer. I know I'm a talented painter. I know I can speak three languages and am going to attend a really nice college someday. Who cares if I get skipped over one time a year for the talent show? After all, I should have read my e-mails."

"Yes, young man, you should've. But, it seems to me your school is not reaching out to the entire student body the way it needs to when students are being celebrated . . . . Tell me, what other special events are set aside to honor students from all disciplines and backgrounds across the building?"

"Mainly, it's just pep rallies and sports stuff . . . . academic team some, band, cheerleaders."

"And Martin, all of that is a good start, and the school should be commended. I simply have reservations, however, that the equity is not where it should be. Am I making sense?"

"Sort of . . . So, you're saying if it's mainly the same kids who are honored and recognized all the time, there's something missing."

"Yes. That's exactly what I'm saying. And I'm sure it's not even noticed by the administration. Your father and I know those folks, and they're good, good people . . . . But, their rituals to celebrate student achievement and successes are too limited."

"We talked about this some in my social studies class, Mom. It's called implicit bias. But, I thought that was an ethnic thing."

"Often it is, Martin. But it goes so much deeper than that. If students are being excluded based on arbitrary rules that marginalize them in some sort of 'rites of passage' that is enjoyed only by the kids who are athletes, wow, that's backward thinking, and I guarantee your classmates who aren't athletes get so, so tired of it . . . Right?"

"Yes, they do. They make fun of the rich kid athletes all the time, too. Call them names."

"And Son, that's not right either . . . . See what a toxic mess the school is endorsing?"

"Yes . . . I get it. May I mention your opinion the next time the topic comes up in social studies?"

"Well, indeed you better! Now, off to school kid . . . Love you Martin."

"Love you Mom."

Questions for Further Reflection:

1. Khalifa's, *et al.*, (2016) research synthesis suggests that school leaders must promote culturally responsive environments through resisting exclusionary practice; promoting inclusivity; recognizing indigenous youth identities; and integrating student culture in all aspects of schooling. Discuss ways in which you, as a school leader, might promote each of the above.
2. How might you guard against your own biases that negatively influence your role as a school leader?
3. What examples of institutional bias have you observed?

NOTES

1. Muhammad A. Khalifa, Mark Anthony Gooden, and James Earl Davis, "Culturally Responsive School Leadership: A Synthesis of the Literature," Review of Educational Research 86, no. 4 (2016): 1274.

2. Khalifa, et al., "Synthesis of Literature," 1277.

3. Khalifa, et al., "Synthesis of Literature," 1272.

Chapter 4

Curriculum, Instruction, and Assessment

Stephanie Sullivan

We think too much about effective methods of teaching and not enough about effective methods of learning.

—John Carolus S.J.[1]

Standard 4: Effective educational leaders develop and support intellectually rigorous and coherent systems of curriculum, instruction, and assessment to promote each student's academic success and well-being.

a) *Implement coherent systems of curriculum, instruction, and assessment that promote the mission, vision, and core values of the school, embody high expectations for student learning, align with academic standards, and are culturally responsive.*

In previous decades, when every classroom had textbooks, it was simple to align curriculum because a school would adopt a textbook series for school-wide implementation. However, we now are in an environment where there may be no textbooks in a school. The instruction may be delivered through various modes of technology, such as online curricula, web-based programs, and distance learning platforms.

So, how do school leaders ensure coherent systems of curriculum that align to the mission, vision, and core values, embody high expectations, and are culturally responsive in this environment? The answer—communication and collaboration. It is important for the school leader to communicate with the various grade-level and content-area teachers, while also providing opportunities for collaboration between grade levels and across disciplines. The school leader must carefully implement the School Based Decision Making (SBDM) policy that was adopted to determine curriculum, needs assessment, and curriculum development and responsibilities according to *KRS 158.6453 (19)*.

Additionally, using only whole group instruction is no longer the norm. Small group instruction, providing differentiation to meet students' needs, is a common practice that requires an entirely new set of curriculum and resources. Utilizing the Response to Intervention (RtI) process employs evidence-based strategies to assist struggling students. Other students, however, may be ready for advanced learning through acceleration and enrichment activities. Therefore, a teacher must navigate through the vast amount of resources available to create and implement a curriculum that meets learners' needs, while aligning to state academic standards.

Leaders must guide teachers to use multiple sources of data to inform instruction based on students' needs. Teachers must be able to determine if remediation is needed for a particular standard or whether students have mastered that concept and are ready to progress. Consistent assessment and analysis are important to ensure teachers are equipped with the knowledge of student understanding to properly plan lessons and design instruction to meet students' needs.

In regard to instruction, effective leaders should be sharing research and promoting best practices in the classroom. Teachers approach instruction in a multitude of ways, utilizing many different teaching methods, but are the strategies they are applying the most effective? When sharing evidence-based practices through embedded professional development, conducting frequent classroom visits, and providing feedback and coaching, instructional leaders can ensure teachers are utilizing best practices that will have the greatest impact on student achievement.

School leaders must make certain students are being taught the standards for their particular subject and grade level and are being provided intervention for those standards that they struggle to master. Schools must focus on standards-based teaching, standards-based assessments, and standards-based reporting. The focus on standards places emphasis on mastery of content, rather than simply a grade. This type of reporting informs teachers, parents, and students of the standards the student has mastered, those that the student is ready to learn, and those for which the student needs intervention.

While teachers may implement different assessments in their class-rooms, there does need to be some consistency within the school. The assessments must target the identified standards for particular grade levels and subjects. Progress monitoring must include administering common assessments at agreed-upon testing windows during the school year to provide an overview of how students are performing. While common assessments may be teacher designed, computer-based formative assess-ments provide normative data and detailed reports that can be used in professional learning communities to discuss student progress and growth. How effectively school leaders utilize that data to inform instruction can greatly impact student learning.

b) *Align and focus systems of curriculum, instruction, and assessment within and across grade levels to promote student academic success, love of learning, the identities and habits of learners, and healthy sense of self.*

Teachers have some academic freedom regarding what and how they teach in their individual classroom; however, the school leader, in collaboration with teacher leaders, should determine what should be consistent school-wide. For example, if fourth grade students are expected to have a goal of earning 100 Accelerated Reader points with 90 percent comprehension, but fifth-grade students are only expected to earn 50 points with 80 percent comprehension, students may experience resentment that *the rules are not fair.* When the rules are not consistent and appropriate for all students, discouragement can occur and hinder the love of learning.

Likewise, if the school creates a school-wide plan for goal attainment, yet some grade-level teachers enforce the expectations while others discredit it, students will receive mixed messages and quickly lose motivation. An effec-tive school leader must communicate the importance of school-wide efforts and ensure that all members of the school staff share the commitment to suc-cessful and consistent implementation.

Another area that may be necessary as a school-wide policy pertains to the amount of homework assigned. For a family that has children in different grade levels, who are assigned vastly different amounts of work, the love for learning can be hampered by the inequity. The child, who spends hours on homework each afternoon while the other is outside playing, may very likely develop resentment, rather than a love of learning.

How a teacher interacts with a student in the classroom will greatly influence the child's healthy, or unhealthy, sense of self. Does the teacher quietly reprimand students or make a spectacle in front of others? When a student does not answer a question correctly, does the teacher humiliate or chastise the child, or prompt and encourage? Through observation, school leaders can monitor interactions and make recommendations as needed. An effective school leader has the courage to confront situations that can negatively impact a student's love of learning and a healthy sense of self. It may also be necessary to bring issues to the SBDM council to create and/or revise the policies as needed.

c) *Promote instructional practice that is consistent with knowledge of child learning and development, effective pedagogy, and the needs of each student.*

This element is most evident in the elementary setting, especially during the primary years. Preschool teachers understand the importance of teaching to the whole child as they understand children develop and grow at different stages and ages. What one child is ready to understand may take longer for another child to comprehend. Additionally, the life experiences and vocabulary which children are exposed to prior to school entry can also impact a child's school readiness. Throughout P-12 education, educators should be aware of child learning and development. Therefore, effective leaders must ensure teachers provide the differentiation and learning experiences that meet the wide range of student needs and abilities within their classroom.

To promote instructional practices that meet the various needs of all students, effective leaders must provide the support teachers need. This can come in many forms, including professional development, coaching, instructional resources, and support staff. Assigning mentors for new teachers, creating co-teaching environments, and encouraging peer observations can provide invaluable support and modeling of best practices to promote effective pedagogy.

d) *Ensure instructional practice that is intellectually challenging, authentic to student experiences, recognizes student strengths, and is differentiated and personalized.*

It is much easier to follow a textbook, page by page, teaching to the whole group, but is that what is best for students? Absolutely not. No two students are the same, so it is imperative that differentiated and personalized instruction is provided. An effective leader can help encourage this practice by creating a schedule that has intentional time devoted to different types of instruction such as whole group, small group, remediation or acceleration, and even problem- or project-based learning.

By providing regular formative assessment in the form of bell-ringers, exit slips, and continual class monitoring, teachers can ensure that instruction is appropriately challenging. If the majority of the class correctly answers all of the bell-ringers, then the majority of the class does not need to sit through a lesson teaching that concept. Effective leaders must expect teachers to have varied lessons, providing small group and differentiated instruction, to meet all students' needs. Modeling, providing professional development, purchasing supplemental materials, securing technology resources, and scheduling staff are some ways leaders can provide the support necessary for teachers to ensure instructional practices that promote student learning.

e) *Promote the effective use of technology in the service of teaching and learning.*

Technology can be used in most all areas of teaching and learning, including planning, instruction, assessment, and reporting. For teachers to implement technology efficiently, and with success, it is important to provide adequate training. Many schools have evolved from a computer room shared among the entire school to a mobile cart that can be reserved for classroom use to a 1-1 device for every student to participate in distance learning. As computer accessibility and diversity increase, effective leaders must ensure teachers are provided the training to utilize all aspects of technology implementation proficiently.

There must be a careful balance of providing an adequate amount of training, without moving into the arena of information overload, and that balance point will vary for different teachers. While some teachers may feel quite comfortable with technology and are ready to be challenged, others will need more guidance and support. Effective leaders should employ innovative techniques to ensure both teacher and student needs are being met through the use of technology.

f) *Employ valid assessments that are consistent with knowledge of child learning and development and technical standards of measurement.*

It does not matter how much time and money is spent on curriculum and instruction, if it is not followed by assessment. Without assessment, student growth and achievement is just assumed, not proved. A teacher can believe a student is learning the intended content, but without assessment data, it cannot be known.

It is important to employ a school-wide assessment tool that is teacher, student, and parent friendly. Reports must provide the data needed to assist teachers in determining which standards students have mastered and which standards they are ready to learn. The effective leader must model how to use assessment data to develop lessons that address student needs. This modeling can take place during regularly scheduled professional learning communities dedicated to using data to drive instruction.

g) *Use assessment data appropriately and within technical limitations to monitor student progress and improve instruction.*

Although a school-wide assessment tool may be utilized, it is of no value if it is not being used to inform instruction to meet students' needs. An effective school leader MUST provide a dedicated time to review data and have discussions regarding student achievement, student growth, mastery of standards, and interventions/accommodations required for student success. The leader should have a system established for data review, including modeling of various reports to guide instructional decisions. As W. Edwards Deming stated, "Without data, you're just another person with an opinion."

SCENARIO

Principal Anderson had the privilege of establishing a new school, with teachers transferring from the other schools within the district and students being assigned to the school through redistricting. The staff were provided the choice of whether or not to transfer to the new school, and those who decided to move were excited about a new start. They were optimistic and motivated to make the school highly successful.

Teachers were allowed the opportunity to teach in new and innovative ways. They dedicated many hours before and after school, working with students. The positive school culture was undeniable. At the end of the year, as state testing was beginning, everyone hoped for the best, since there were no prior state assessment scores with which to compare.

When the test scores were published in the fall, the staff was thrilled that the school received proficient scores. With that success, teachers continued to do what they had done the year before. Teachers worked diligently trying to reach each child, and children were motivated to do their best. This success continued year after year, until one year, the scores came back in the "Needs Improvement" category. WOW, what had happened? Teachers had done nothing differently than they had in previous years. Yes, there were some new teachers, but for the most part, teachers had taught like they always had. So, why did they not have the same results?

The entire school was deflated. They had never experienced this type of failure. Principal Anderson called a colleague in a neighboring district to share the disappointing news. She explained that she just didn't understand what happened. The colleague asked, "What did your formative data show you as you were progress monitoring last year?" Anderson was at a loss. Data? What data? Yes, some of the primary teachers had administered the STAR assessment in their classrooms, but those results were never discussed. All of a sudden, a sense of realization occurred. Anderson thought, "I haven't been using data. I have failed my students and staff. I never realized that was something I should be doing. I assumed since we had been experiencing success in previous years, we would naturally continue that success."

The next day, Principal Anderson went to the board office to speak with the Instructional Supervisor and Technology Coordinator. They discussed how STAR was available for all the elementary schools in the district, and they agreed to model how to use the reports with the staff in the Professional Learning Community (PLC) meetings. Anderson went back to the office and immediately created a new schedule that allowed an extra planning on Fridays for dedicated data review. During the grade-level PLC meetings the students would be supervised by the counselor, family resource coordinator, or assistant principal for special instruction—such as Drug Abuse Resistance Education (DARE), character development, and guest speakers—to allow the time needed for teachers to engage in data analysis. These meetings would be held every Friday, except on the last Friday of the month when school-wide assemblies were conducted.

On that first Friday, the central office representative attended and modeled how to use the data report. Copies were provided for the teachers, along with binders to keep an organized data system for monitoring student progress. Highlighters were provided, and teachers engaged in identifying students reaching benchmark and those needing Tier 2 or Tier 3 interventions. Week after week, various reports in math and reading were reviewed, and teachers began to truly understand the needs of their students.

Teachers revised lesson plans for the upcoming week and re-taught standards that students had not mastered, and Principal Anderson altered schedules to allow for dedicated intervention time and strategically scheduled aides to grade levels to provide small group instruction. It wasn't long until Anderson was able to lead the PLC meetings herself. Teachers soon were excited for the next formative testing window to see how much their students had grown, and students had their own monitoring system and were anxious to show improvement from their previous scores.

When the Kentucky Performance Rating for Educational Progress (K-PREP) test scores were received the following fall, the school had amazingly gone from a "Needs Improvement" status to a "School of Distinction," ranking 42nd out of over 700 elementary schools across the state. Although there was great excitement at this tremendous gain in student learning, some wondered if scores were elevated due to the "growth" component from being so low the previous year. The school, however, was motivated to continue using assessment to drive instructional change. The following year, state scores once again reflected a "School of Distinction," with an increased ranking of thirty-sixth in the state. The following year, the school ranked twelfth in the state, and the following year it was recognized as a Blue-Ribbon School of Excellence.

This success story is all about the importance of data. Did the teachers work any harder during those last three years than they had the previous ten years? No, they worked smarter. Without using data, teachers didn't truly know what students needed or what they were ready to learn. Also, it shows that Principal Anderson was willing to learn from others. She had experienced failure and reached out to others to help her grow, which had a profound impact on student learning. Is a test score the most important thing on which a principal should focus? No, but that score is a reflection of student learning. Anderson's only regret is that she did not learn the importance of using assessment to promote student success and well-being sooner in her educational career.

Effective Instructional School Leaders:

- provide a dedicated time, beyond planning, for Professional Learning Communities to review data on a regular basis.
- implement a data system for collection (such as data notebooks, data walls, electronic files, etc.).
- model and lead PLCs to use data to inform instructional practice.
- identify student needs (achievement, growth, tier interventions, etc.).
- follow classroom observations with feedback to ensure instructional practices are based on data.

Questions for Further Reflection:

1. As an effective instructional leader, how will you ensure teachers are meeting the learning needs of their students?
2. What is evidence of coherent systems of curriculum and instruction in your school? How could you improve these systems as a leader?
3. How will you promote a data-driven focus for instruction? What supports will you provide as an instructional leader?
4. In what ways can technology enhance teaching and learning? What are innovative approaches that you would model and promote as an instructional leader?

NOTE

1. John Carolus, Retrieved from https://www.activityvillage.co.uk/teacher-quotes.

Chapter 5

Community of Care and Support for Students

Rosemarie Young

Every child deserves a champion—an adult who will never give up on them, who understands the power of connection and insists that they become the best that they can possibly be.

—Rita Pierson

Standard 5: Effective educational leaders cultivate an inclusive, caring, and supportive school community that promotes the academic success and well-being of each student.

This is the heart and soul of the school, and the school leader must keep this as the focus of the work of the school. Children often come to school with multiple issues that affect their ability to concentrate and learn. There is much guidance available to help schools understand this critical mission and support their work to provide a supportive, inclusive, and caring environment for each student.

The Learning Policy Institute provides a number of key findings in its publication "Educating the Whole Child: Improving School Climate to Support Student Success."[1] The publication stresses that there is variability in human development and adversity affects learning. Learning in schools includes social, emotional, and academic learning. The good news is that development is malleable and can be greatly supported by building human relationships through establishing catalysis for healthy development and learning. The Institute reinforces that children construct knowledge based on experiences, relationships, and social contexts.

43

Critical to the success of building identity-safe classrooms are four elements:

- Promoting understanding, student voice, student responsibility, and classroom community;
- Cultivating diversity as a resource for teaching;
- Building trusting classroom relationships based on positive interactions; and
- Establishing caring, orderly, purposeful classrooms.[2]

Consequently, the Institute makes four strong recommendations for school leaders in building a productive school environment:

- Build a positive school climate in both classrooms and the school as a whole.
- Shape positive student behavior through social and emotional learning.
- Develop productive instructional strategies that support motivation, competence, and self-directed learning.
- Create individualized supports that address student needs, including the effects of trauma and adversity.[3]

The elements of this PSEL standard speak clearly to the need to establish caring communities for students.

a) *Build and maintain a safe, caring, and healthy school environment that meets the academic, social, emotional, and physical needs of each student.*

Schools must look at the needs of the whole student and provide whatever is necessary for each student to thrive in the school community. Certainly, the safety and well-being of each child is a major responsibility of the school leader. Within this community, the school leader must also build the programs and services to address academic, social, emotional and physical learning needs of students.

Academic supports must be provided for all levels of need, including remediation, gifted/talented/advanced, special needs, and diverse learners. A range of emotional and social offerings serve to support the wide range of needs of students for healthy development. Programs that support the physical needs of students can help to ensure a healthy lifestyle during their adult years. The school leader must build a coherent system of programs and services and consistently assess those programs to determine if they are meeting students' needs. A needs assessment can be an invaluable tool to provide guidance for the services and programs offered to students.

b) *Create and sustain a school environment in which each student is known, accepted and valued, trusted and respected, cared for, and encouraged to be an active and responsible member of the school community.*

This is a critical responsibility for school leaders. Klem and Connell[4] have noted that as many as 40–60 percent of all students in urban, suburban, and rural communities are chronically disengaged from school by the time they reach high school. Individuals who feel connected and valued are more likely to thrive in the school setting and develop resiliency skills.

In looking at the research literature across the different fields of inquiry, Blum[5] found three school characteristics that support young people to feel connected to school while encouraging student achievement. These are (1) high academic standards coupled with strong teacher support; (2) an environment in which adult and student relationships are positive and respectful; and (3) a physically and emotionally safe school environment.

Many schools have developed a mentoring program for their students and have recruited staff members to follow students through their time in the school. The National Mentoring Resource Center[6] has developed a number of resources to support the development of effective mentoring programs.

c) *Provide coherent systems of academic and social supports, services, extracurricular activities, and accommodations to meet the range of learning needs of each student.*

Schools are becoming more and more diverse, with students requiring greater support to meet the academic expectations required. According to Quinn and Fullan,[7] coherence is "the shared depth of understanding about the nature of the work." Quinn and Fullan have developed a coherent framework consisting of the following four components, with schools' leaders being the glue connecting and integrating them:

- focusing direction, which builds collective purpose;
- cultivating collaborative cultures, which develops capacity;
- deepening learning, which accelerates improvement and innovation; and
- securing accountability based on capacity built from the inside out.[8]

d) *Promote adult-student, student-peer, and school-community relationships that value and support academic learning and positive social and emotional development.*

This particular element supports the other elements already discussed. The Collaborative for Academic, Social, and Emotional Learning (CASEL) has done a great deal of research around social and emotional learning (SEL) in schools and has developed a number of resources to support schools in this work. According to CASEL,[9] "a systemic, schoolwide approach to SEL intentionally cultivates a caring, participatory, and equitable learning environment and evidence-based practices that actively involve all students in their social, emotional, and academic growth."

e) *Cultivate and reinforce student engagement in school and positive student conduct.* Positive Behavioral Interventions and Supports (PBIS) has been implemented in a number of schools. According to the Center on PBIS,[10] "PBIS is an evidence-based three-tiered framework to improve and integrate all of the data, systems, and practices affecting student outcomes every day. PBIS creates schools where all students succeed." In addition, implementation of PBIS promotes a culture of equity and effectiveness while improving the social, emotional, and academic outcomes for all students.

Schools must consider the individual needs of each student and support that student's growth and achievement. To this end, the school leader must strive to establish a school community that values the engagement of every student and structure the school environment so that students are supported in developing strong, positive behaviors in the school community

f) *Infuse the school's learning environment with the cultures and languages of the school's community.*

The National Association of Elementary School Principals (NAESP) established a diversity task force to examine and identify effective practices that promote culturally responsive schools. In this guide, the task force identified four leadership competencies and recommendations to achieve the competencies. The four competencies are:

1. Advance Culturally Responsive Leadership
2. Diversify Student and Adult Capacity to Transform Schools
3. Utilize Assets to Ensure Culturally Responsive Teaching
4. Provide Diverse Opportunities for All Students

Likewise, the National Association of Secondary School Principals (NASSP)[11] has developed a position statement on culturally responsive schools that contains recommendations for school leaders. NASSP has developed the Diversity Responsive Principal Tool that can be used to determine whether the school leader has implemented policies and practices that enhance the academic success of students of diverse racial, ethnic, cultural, and linguistic backgrounds.

Developing a school culture that nurtures the academic, social, emotional, and physical needs of each student is a key responsibility of school leaders. When this happens, it becomes a school that values its students and believes in the power of building effective relationships to guide students to reaching their true potential. In the end, this should be the mission of every school.

SCENARIO

Martha Wilson has been appointed as the principal of Hopewell Middle School. Before she began the position, Dr. Thomas, the superintendent, met with her to discuss issues she needed to address immediately. Dr. Thomas related that the previous principal had been there for approximately nine years. In the beginning, the principal was effective but had become overwhelmed and let a number of issues slide.

The superintendent felt the school had become too adult oriented and the focus needed to return to the students and their needs. She had also received a number of complaints from parents who felt their children had been treated unfairly by teachers and administration. The superintendent ended the meeting by requesting Martha to return to meet with her in one month to discuss her progress in addressing the issues.

Martha had four weeks before the start of the new school year. She realized she needed to delve deeper into the culture and programming of the school. One of the first things she did was to meet with the teachers, staff, students, and parents. Meeting with the grade-level teacher teams first, she realized that each team had its' own set of expectations, and some were not so student friendly. One team, though, stood out to her with their focus on meeting students' needs and with their flexibility to adjust to student needs.

Student groups shared that some teachers were great (loved the teachers on the team with the flexibility), but some were rigid and didn't seem to care if they were in class or not. They shared that they felt students were treated differently by some teachers—with some being targeted by certain teachers. These remarks came from students not being targeted.

The parents were pretty much on the same page but added that some teachers would not meet with them and only called when there was a problem.

Martha knew she had a great deal of work to do but she needed to put some systems and actions into place right away. She asked the flexible team's team leader, Sam, to a meeting. She also invited teachers from other teams who seemed to be more flexible in their thinking. In this gathering, she was open and honest about the issues and the need to make changes. Together, they talked about a vision of what the school could be and brainstormed what would be needed to make the vision happen.

Martha asked the group if they would be willing to meet with some students and parents to hear their thoughts. Sam was the first to embrace this collaboration, as he understood it was essential to the success of the school. Martha asked if those present would be willing to serve on a School Renewal committee with her. All accepted. It certainly helped that Martha was so passionate about the vision of what the school could be and that they would be in this together.

After two weeks of meeting with students, parents, and community members, the committee developed a strategic plan to arrive at the vision as well as some action steps for the start of the school year. They worked immediately on developing school-wide expectations for student behavior and guidelines for teachers to follow. They also looked at services provided to the students and realized that they were not being offered equitably or in a consistent manner. Again, guidelines were developed and some additional support systems were put in place. Martha was thrilled with the work and realized that she had outstanding teachers who just needed to be empowered to do what was right. She also realized that there was much more to be done, but they had a roadmap and the passion to make the needed changes. Going home that night, she hoped the next morning's meeting with the superintendent would go well. It did!

Caring Leaders:

- advocate for students, staff, parents, and the community.
- build a "culture of care" in the school community.
- protect those who can least protect themselves.
- listen to all stakeholders with empathy and respect.
- model for others how to build a relationship-driven school.
- put people over programs.
- focus on what's best for each student, seeing the potential and believing in the growth mindset.

Questions for Further Reflection:

1. What programs, resources, and systems are in place that support the emotional, social, academic, and physical development of my students?
2. How do I know that each student is named and claimed and supported throughout the student's school experience in my school?
3. What range of services and programs are needed in my school to provide academic and social support, extracurricular activities, and accommodations to meet the learning needs of each student?
4. How can I model and instill relationships among students, adults, and the community that support and value academic learning as well as positive social and emotional development?

5. How do I cultivate a climate in my school where each student is engaged, and we are focused on positive student conduct?
6. How do I infuse the school's learning environment with the cultures and languages of my school's community in a meaningful way?
7. How do I ensure all programs and services are provided in a coherent system of supports for students?

NOTES

1. Linda Darling-Hammond and Channa Cook-Harvey, *Educating the Whole Child: Improving School Climate to Support Students* (Palo Alto, CA: Learning Policy Institute, 2018).

2. Darling-Hammond and Cook-Harvey, *Educating Whole Child*, p. 21.

3. Darling-Hammond and Cook-Harvey, *Educating Whole Child*, p. 14.

4. Adam Klen and James Connell, "Relationships Matter: Linking Teacher Support to Student Engagement and Achievement," *Journal of School Health* 74, no. 7 (2004): 262.

5. Robert Blum, "A Case for School Connectedness," *Educational Leadership* 62 no. 7 (2005): 16–20.

6. The National Mentoring Center, 2016, Retrieved from https://www.mentoring.org/new-site/wp-content/uploads/2016/03/Success-Mentors-School-Checklist.FINAL_.pdf.

7. Michael Fullan and Joanne Quinn, "Coherence Making: How Leaders Cultivate the Pathway for School and System Change with a Shared Process," *School Administrator* (June 2016): 30.

8. Michael Fullan and Joanne Quinn, "Coherence Making," p. 32.

9. CASEL What is Social and Emotional Learning? Retrieved from https://schoolguide.casel.org/what-is-sel/what-is-sel/.

10. Positive Behavior Intervention and Supports. Information located at https://www.pbis.org/.

11. National Association of Secondary School Principals, "Position Statement: Culturally Responsive Schools," Retrieved from https://www.nassp.org/policy-advocacy-center/nassp-position-statements/culturally-responsive-schools/ (2019): 5–6.

Chapter 6

Professional Capacity of School Personnel

Michael Kessinger

Leadership is affirming people's worth and potential so clearly that they are inspired to see it in themselves.

—Stephen Covey

Standard 6: Effective educational leaders develop the professional capacity and practice of school personnel to promote each student's academic success and well-being.

a) *Recruit, hire, support, develop, and retain effective and caring teachers and other professional staff and form them into an educationally effective faculty.*

Not only is it important to seek out well-trained teachers who will meet the instructional needs of students, but also to find individuals to serve in other positions that will form an effective and efficient faculty in the school. No new teacher comes into a school knowing what it will take to help all students to be successful. There is not a student teacher that has been exposed to all the possible challenges one will find once they have obtained their first teaching position. This is especially true when a new teacher is coming from another area or a different region of the nation. The culture, climate, and distinct personality of faculty, staff, and students are different in every school.

When looking at applicants to fill a vacancy, the educational leader must take the opportunity to clearly examine the qualifications of an individual to determine if they will be a good fit to the community to address the mission and vision of the school.

Having a well-developed induction and mentoring program within the school with teachers to help shape new individuals is essential. No new teacher should be "thrown to the wolves" and be placed, essentially, in isolation from those who can help the new teacher develop into a successful team member. There is so much to learn during the first few years in the profession. New employees need to be mentored in a way to enable them to be successful in their position.

Teachers and other professional staff could eventually look for changes in their placement either within the district, or outside to another district. Some will also reach the time of retirement and regardless of the situation, a replacement will be needed. The effective educational leader must proactively plan for those situations when a new replacement will be needed. You cannot just wait for the vacancy to occur and then start planning on looking for a replacement. You have to look ahead and plan especially when a retirement is anticipated.

b) *Plan for and manage staff turnover and succession, providing opportunities for effective induction and mentoring of new personnel.*

Planning for replacing a teacher or professional staff that might resign or transfer to another school can start when you are seeing the "writing on the walls." An individual who is unhappy in their current position will let others know of it. Their attendance, involvement in various school activities, and comments in teacher meetings all point to the potential of a vacancy occurring. An effective educational leader has to be prepared for the unexpected and be ready to begin the process to seek out a replacement. Then the cycle starts over again to further develop the individuals to be effective members of the school community.

c) *Develop teachers' and staff members' professional knowledge, skills, and practice through differentiated opportunities for learning and growth, guided by an understanding of professional and adult learning and development.*

One of the many challenges of an educational leader is to constantly build upon the capacity of the teachers and other professional staff. It is not wise for one to believe that "now that I'm hired, I'm done learning." Constant changes in the educational process demand that opportunities be provided for professionals to enhance their skills and capacities to meet the demands of student achievement.

The recent events surrounding Covid-19 have created the need for teachers to be prepared to address the challenges of virtual instruction. No one could have predicted schools would be closing their doors and that students would need to be taught completely over the internet and in virtual meetings. No preparation program in the past has provided the opportunities for teachers to gain the skills needed to pull off a change in such a short period of time.

The possibilities for fall 2020 of the various ways the school would operate created a need for educational leaders to have a vision of what the future might look like. Multiple professional development sessions to address the needs of teachers to deliver instruction along with meeting the academic needs of students had to be considered and presented. Since teachers possess knowledge and skill sets different from one another, a one-size-fits-all approach cannot be used. The effective leader must take into consideration what various opportunities exist and help direct each teacher toward the most appropriate training.

Providing the training opportunities is only one aspect of helping teachers and professional staff to continuously grow. The effective educational leader must also monitor, evaluate, and provide feedback regarding the professional development attended. Observing the impact of trainings upon the instructional practices can further assist teachers and staff to grow professionally. Once new knowledge is obtained, there has to be refinement of the skills and additional experiences provided. Teachers and staff not only need to practice the new skills, but they also need feedback of how to further shape the knowledge, so it naturally occurs in the work setting.

d) *Foster continuous improvement of individual and collective instructional capacity to achieve outcomes envisioned for each student.*

Communication of expectations by the school leader is a key for success. Teacher needs are typically documented on an evaluation feedback summary report. The needs for growth, the areas needing further refinement, and the impact on student learning all become part of a well-designed evaluation system. The educational leader must provide teachers and staff with anticipated outcomes from attending training sessions and then monitor the impact of those professional learning opportunities.

Gone are the days when once a teacher was hired, they are left alone. In today's changing world, the effective educational leader must take an active role in the acquisition of new knowledge and skills by teachers and professional staff. Once the acquisition has occurred, then there is a monitoring and evaluation of the implementation and impact of the new abilities upon student achievement. Training should not be attended just to meet employment requirements. Training must be purposeful, address a previously established purpose, and be evaluated on the effectiveness of meeting the needs of the teacher and the needs of the students.

e) *Deliver actionable feedback about instruction and other professional practice through valid, research-anchored systems of supervision and evaluation to support the development of teachers' and staff members' knowledge, skills, and practice.*

Evaluations play an important part in improving the professional skills, knowledge, and practices. The most important component of any evaluation system is the feedback provided after the observation and analysis have occurred. Rather than a "you must do better in getting the students involved in the lesson," the feedback must provide suggestions of what could be done to accomplish the goal. It is showing the teacher how to improve their skills rather than just saying they have to change what they do.

For effective and actionable feedback to happen, the effective educational leader needs to keep abreast of current trends identified in the literature. By reading professional journals, attending professional regional, state, and national conferences, the leader can gain important awareness of ways to help teachers and professional staff to improve their practices.

And it is important to note that evaluations are not the only way for the feedback to occur. Building walkthroughs with a few minutes observing what is happening in the classroom can also provide the building administrator with data by which to have appropriate conversations with the educators. Daily supervision is a requirement of building leaders to ensure teachers and others are not only doing their job but are doing their job with efficiency and effectiveness.

f) *Empower and motivate teachers and staff to the highest levels of professional practice and to continuous learning and improvement.*

Allowing education professionals to have the power to select what trainings and professional development they will attend is a challenge in today's education economic times. Budgets are tight, resources are few, and enabling teachers to go where needed to gain skills they need to do an outstanding job requires planning and opportunities. Of course, administrators have to be careful not to give opportunities to one and not to others. Fairness is the name of the game.

When a teacher is told they need to gain a particular skill, the effective leader provides the means for the teacher to gain that skill. Encouraging and motivating teachers and staff to perform at their highest levels includes providing opportunities to gain the knowledge needed to do a great job for students. This might require the creative use of funds and the long-term planning to be able to support the needs of teachers. You can empower and motivate with words, but as the cliché states, "Actions speak louder than words." Provide opportunities for teachers to meet their professional needs and their actions will increase their professional practice.

g) *Develop the capacity, opportunities, and support for teacher leadership and leadership from other members of the school community.*

Shared leadership is the big word in today's education setting—no more of the authoritarian leader that rules with an iron fist. Conversations are held with teachers and professional staff to have a voice in decisions made for the whole school. Leadership opportunities are offered to all stakeholders. The effective educational leader seeks feedback from others to help support the mission and vision of the school. The word in today's world is transparency. Nothing is hidden, and everything is out in the open.

To help build the capacity of other stakeholders, the leader must have an open-door policy. It is permissible to disagree, but it is not appropriate to ignore the thoughts of others. Asking questions, seeking advice, bouncing ideas off others, and considering the implications of decisions are all concepts that promote the building of teacher leadership capacity.

One successful approach is to empower others to be in charge of a particular situation. The building principal does not need to be involved with the planning of the junior prom. Nor do they need to have absolute control in the adoption of textbooks, curriculum changes, or scheduling. Those and other responsibilities can be put in the control of committees and teacher leaders. By allowing others to make decisions, you are enabling them to build their capacity to lead and to make a difference.

h) *Promote the personal and professional health, well-being, and work-life balance of faculty and staff.*

For many new teachers, especially those new to the community, volunteering for every school event seems to become a personal, internal expectation. Hoping to keep their job for the next school year, an employee wants to show their face not only to the students and community but also to the administration. Attending every sporting event and every class meeting, going to every school and district meeting, and volunteering to help with all fund-raising events becomes a pattern for many new teachers. Being at every school happening can put unnecessary concerns upon the individual's work-life balance.

The effective educational leader will sometimes need to have a sit-down chat with a professional employee. A nice conversation about "not overdoing it" is sometimes needed. The teachers that stay out late every night at every school event will not be able to give their best in the classroom.

Not only is it important for a balance to exist between work and personal life, there needs to be opportunities given to employees by the educational leader that promote both personal and professional health. This sometimes will involve opportunities to do something during the workday. For example, an employee who needs to get the annual flu shot during the school day could have the principal volunteer to fill-in for a few minutes in the classroom. Or a teacher that needs to leave a few minutes early for a dentist appointment might not need to fill out a "sick-leave card." Know that little things such as this show the employees the education leader cares about them not only professionally, but personally.

i) *Tend to their own learning and effectiveness through reflection, study, and improvement, maintaining a healthy work-life balance.*

One day the new superintendent walked into the high school and told the secretary he wanted to see the building principal. It was a Friday, and the attitude of the superintendent seemed serious. The secretary looked at the superintendent, with a little puzzled look, and said, "It's Friday, he's on the football field." The superintendent was now the one with a confused look and replied, "Why?" Evidently the superintendent was not aware of the tradition the principal had established over the years. "He's lining the field for the game tonight. He always does that on game night. I really think it's a way for him to get away and get his mind straight from all the things that happened this week." The superintendent gave a thoughtful look—"Maybe I need to go help him."

Not only do educational leaders need to be concerned with their own professional improvement by attending regional and state meetings, but they also need to be concerned about their own well-being. The actual Friday situation presented was a tradition for this building principal for the fifteen years he served in the position. It was a way for him to maintain a healthy work-life balance. Over the years, he was asked many times why he did that—why would he do something the maintenance or the athletic department could have accomplished? His response was always consistent, "It gives me time to think about everything else that is going on in my school. It helps me to relax."

There is so much change occurring in our educational system. Effective leaders must keep abreast of the new directions the system is going, and there has to be time to just think about things. Covid-19 has resulted in significant changes in the administrator's role. Now they are learning new ways of delivering instruction using online resources and procedures. The school leader, to be effective to his staff and teachers, must take opportunities to expand on their own capacity as an educator, as a mentor for the faculty, and as a school leader. The effective building leader does not sit behind a closed door, but rather gets out and continues to build their skills and knowledge to best serve the whole school community.

SCENARIO

A spring break trip out of state was just what Gary needed. It had been a hard semester with getting ready for student teaching in the fall. Gary and a few of his friends drove the 680 miles to his grandparents' house. After a few days visiting, the crew packed up and drove another 240 miles to a little town where Gary's relatives lived. He had a job interview for a teaching position—his first invite to discuss a job opening.

The interview was very interesting. Gary only met with the superintendent, Mr. Jones. The forty-five-minute conversation had questions about Gary's background, and there was very little about teaching philosophy, methods, or style. The superintendent did not offer to take Gary to the high school to meet the principal or any of the teachers. It was a one-on-one interview and very short.

A month later, Gary received a letter. He had a job offer. And the superintendent, Mr. Jones, indicated the position would be available after Gary finished his student teaching in mid-October. For whatever reason, Gary accepted the job and started planning on the 794-mile drive to the little town.

Arriving on a brisk October morning at the school at 7:15 a.m., Gary went to the office. There was no one there. So he took a seat. Around 7:35 a.m., the secretary showed up. Looking Gary over, she asked, "Can I help you?"

"Yes, I'm Gary Peterson, and I was told to report here."

"What for?" he was asked.

"I'm the new math teacher," he said.

"Oh? We were told but weren't given any information. You will need to wait til the principal gets here," she said.

Waiting until 7:55 a.m., Gary began wondering what he had gotten himself into. They didn't know he was coming. They didn't know much of anything. Gary waited and the principal arrived.

"Mr. Smith, this is Gary Peterson. You know, our new math teacher."

Mr. Smith looked at Gary, and gave a short "Hello, I'll get someone to show you to your classroom." He added, "Oh, you will be moving around, so I'll have someone come and get you at the end of first period."

That was it. No introduction. No "I'll show you around." No, "I'll introduce you to other teachers."

Again, the thought: "What am I doing here?"

By the end of the day, Gary had been to four different classrooms. He was a floater. He had met a few teachers, but the distance they showed him made Gary uncomfortable. Mr. Smith, the principal, did not get back to him at all that first day. There was no attempt to make him feel welcomed, nor to give him a chance to ask questions. It was not what the first day of teaching should be.

Although the first day was very awkward, Gary made it through the week and month. Eventually, he made a few friends in the school and became aware of the inner politics of the organization. The superintendent was a political boss. He controlled everything in the county. Nothing seemed to happen without him knowing about it. The principal, Mr. Smith, had been principal at the old high school before the consolidation. His assistant principal, Mr. Ward, had been principal at the other high school but was not on excellent terms with the superintendent. You could tell there was a little resentment between the two during teacher meetings.

One of the unfortunate things about the school culture was there was no encouragement by the administration in regard to classroom teaching. In fact, Gary never had a visit by either the principal or the assistant principal. They did not have a clue of what he was doing or how he was doing. The other math teachers didn't come by either. Gary was an island—he operated as he saw fit.

It was early February and Gary went to see the principal. "Mr. Smith, there is a meeting in Grayville, and I would really like to attend it. It's on the new textbooks we are getting next year, and the publisher is providing free materials. It would also give me an opportunity to meet other math teachers in the area and to get some ideas of how I might improve my teaching of Algebra I."

"Oh, you don't need to go there. We always get the free materials. Mr. Jones (superintendent) knows the book representative, and he makes sure we get what we need. Besides, you don't need to talk to other math teachers. You're doing okay."

As he finished his sentence, Gary thought, "You haven't been in my classroom, you have no idea what I'm doing," and said, "Ok, I thought I would ask. It seemed like it would be a good thing to do."

He was confused. He didn't understand why Mr. Smith didn't want him to make connections with other math teachers. He didn't know why he didn't want him to do a better job. Gary knew that he was viewed as an "outsider" since he wasn't from the community. But he needed to get some ideas of how he could be a better teacher.

Jumping ahead six years. Gary is still at the same high school. Mr. Smith is no longer principal. He has moved to the central office as an instructional supervisor. Taking his place is another Mr. Smith—a second cousin to the previous Mr. Smith. The new principal had been at an elementary school. Mr. Ward had just retired, and the school needed a new assistant principal. The new principal had heard about Gary and there was a conversation.

"So, Gary, you have your principal papers, right?"

"Yes sir. I've been taking classes, so I can get that pay raise."

"How would you feel about being my assistant principal? It would be a promotion, more days, and more pay. Are you interested?"

"Absolutely. But can I still teach a class—maybe one class a day? I really like teaching."

"I think I can work that into the schedule. Let's go and talk to Mr. Jones."

After the conversation with Mr. Jones, the superintendent agreed that it was time for Gary to assume the role of assistant principal. He was excited, but also worried. How would the rest of the teachers take him being promoted? Would there be resentment of the "outsider" being moved up to a position of authority? How would they react?

The word went around the school quickly. There were congratulations, and there were "How did YOU get that job? You're not even from here!"

Gary knew it was going to be a challenge. He had to do a good job of helping not only Mr. Smith with his duties but also convincing the teachers that he could be helpful to them.

Mr. Smith was changing things at the high school that teachers were not happy about. He was going to do classroom observations. There were going to be teacher evaluations. And the unfortunate part was he was assigning Gary to do some observations also. For some teachers, this was not a happy announcement.

Gary knew what needed to be done, and he treated each teacher professionally and fairly. There was the pre-observation conference. He went over the paperwork, described the process that would be followed, scheduled the day of the observation, and the post-observation conference. He followed the process step by step. No one was going to be able to say he made a difference between any teachers.

For the teachers, they did not like that new approach. Some were used to getting their way. Some resented being observed. There were those that didn't let it bother them. Those were the good teachers that did what they needed to do.

The observations were completed, and the post-observations were conducted. Each teacher was provided with suggestions of how to improve their classroom instruction. Some teachers, especially some of those that resented being evaluated, were told of professional development meetings coming up that they could attend during the school day. In fact, mileage would be paid for them to attend.

The air was buzzing with a lot of conversations. "He wanted to send me to a conference, and he's going to pay for my travel. What is going on? That has never happened before."

Teachers were starting to get the feeling, not just from Gary but also from Mr. Smith, that "someone finally cared about what I did in my classroom." Where were they getting the money? One teacher even asked Gary, "Who did you all rob? We have never had money to pay for gas!"

Gary's response was simple while Mr. Smith smiled on. "Creative use of money. We want to make sure that you get what is needed to make our students perform better. That's it. And how can that happen if you never go anywhere to learn how to do things better? Not saying what you're doing is not good. But I'm sure you will find some ideas that will make it better for students. Isn't that what we are all about? Making it better for our students? Yeah, that's what we're here for."

Equipping Leaders:

- hire those that will help meet the mission and vision of the school.
- provide opportunities to develop skills and knowledge.
- plan for the future in terms of personnel and academic needs.
- hold everyone, including themselves, accountable.
- seek opportunities for professional growth for self and others.
- evaluate and provide actionable feedback to enable growth.
- promote shared leadership with all stakeholders.
- expect and hold others accountable for doing the best they can do.
- make everyone feel like they are part of the "family."
- allow others to make a decision regarding their professional needs.
- are creative in the use of resources and funds to help staff meet their needs.
- seek and promote a balance with work duties and personal life.
- recognize the professional and personal needs of faculty and staff.

- seek to keep knowledgeable of current trends and of effective leadership.
- focus upon the leadership capacity of others.
- make decisions with the students' best interest in mind.

Effective educational leaders seek to build the capacity, knowledge, skills, and professional practices of all teachers and professional staff. Their goal is to have the best professional staff to meet the academic needs of ALL students, regardless of race, ethnicity, gender, or disadvantage or disability. The leader seeks out the best teachers and professional staff and provides them with all the resources and opportunities to continue to grow. The students deserve the "best of the best," and the effective leader does everything possible to make that happen.

Questions for Further Reflection:

1. What areas of school leadership present the most challenge to you in assisting all school personnel to focus on and promote the academic success and well-being of ALL students?
2. What past mentors have had a helpful influence on you in growing into this leadership position?
3. What opportunities have you been provided and have offered to others to help facilitate leadership from various members of the school community?
4. What suggestions would you have for aspiring school leaders to help others and promote the growth of all members of the school community

Chapter 7

Professional Community for Teachers and Staff

Ann H. Burns

Alone we can do so little; together we can do so much.

—Helen Keller

There is immense power when a group of people with similar interests gets together to work toward the same goals.

—Idowu Koyenikan

Standard 7: Effective educational leaders foster a professional community of teachers and other professional staff to promote each student's academic success and well-being.

There has been much written about how school leaders develop a professional community of faculty and staff so that the focus is squarely on student success. A common definition related to professional learning suggests an ongoing process in which educators work collaboratively in regularly scheduled meetings to collectively examine instructional practices and plan intentional actions to achieve better results for each student they serve. These groups of professionals share the belief that to improve learning outcomes for students, teachers must be continuous learners as well.[1]

If the core work of the school is to improve student learning for each student that passes through the doors of the school, then educational leaders must develop the collaborative nature of all faculty and staff to support the collective learning for all. Standard 7 addresses the specific measures for effective professional learning communities for teachers and other professional staff.

a) *Develops workplace conditions for teachers and other professional staff that promote effective professional development, practice and student learning.*

Effective educational leaders understand the importance of "setting the table" for positive working conditions. The best way to understand how to do this is to review prior working conditions data and ask specific questions about the data. Talk with the teachers and staff regarding what makes the school unique and what they need regarding professional development. To improve working conditions, research prior data and what has been done prior to the current work. If there is an outlier in the data, use root cause analysis to discover why the data says what it does.

b) *Empowers and entrusts teachers and staff with collective responsibility for meeting the academic, social, emotional, and physical needs of each student, pursuant to the mission, vision, and core values of the school.*

Schools are collective learning places that include the adults, as well as the students. Each decision related to school improvement should support the mission, vision, and core values of the school. The decisions made collectively by the teachers, staff, parents, and students ensure that all stakeholders have been given a platform to advocate and have input in the learning process. Effective instructional leaders understand the importance of engaging teachers in the learning process.

Committee work becomes an important function of professional processes for schools. Invite the faculty and staff to become a part of the guidance for schools through shared governance of policy implementation. Committees respond to common school issues related to student placement, adoption of curriculum, assessment practices, scheduling of time, and use of school space.

Instructional leaders should include faculty and staff in the decision-making process to create a culture of community focused on learning for all and improvement of student achievement. Develop strategies and a specific plan to involve faculty and staff. Then guide the implementation and monitoring of the progress related to the plan.

c) *Establishes and sustains a professional culture of engagement and commitment to shared vision, goals, and objectives pertaining to the education of the whole child; high expectations for professional work; ethical and equitable practice; trust and open communication; collaboration, collective efficacy, and continuous individual and organizational learning and improvement.*

Effective instructional leaders develop structures for continuous learning and improvement of teachers and staff. What are the long-term plans related to school improvement? How do you develop current teachers? What structures are in place to mentor new hires and marginal faculty and staff? These questions can be addressed through continuous, job-embedded learning for all faculty and staff.

Develop a culture of trust by being a trustworthy leader. To do this, hold all faculty and staff accountable for student achievement and school improvement. How do you develop this culture? By hiring faculty and staff that will embrace the mission, vision, and core values of the school. When one teacher leaves, replace that teacher with another teacher that can support the school mission. The interview process should be designed to find the best-fit candidate for the school culture.

d) *Promotes mutual accountability among teachers and other professional staff for each student's success and the effectiveness of the school as a whole.*

Everyone is responsible for the collective learning and student achievement of all students. The old saying, "You are only as strong as your weakest teacher," is true in this element. During professional collaborative time, all faculty and staff come prepared to work on the work. There is collective efficacy around best practice and student achievement. The culture supports continuous improvement and critical feedback related to individual faculty and staff accountability, student accountability, and school accountability.

e) *Develops and supports open, productive, caring, and trusting working relationships among leaders, faculty, and staff to promote professional capacity and the improvement of practice.*

"People don't care how much you know, until they know how much you care"—Theodore Roosevelt. Effective instructional leaders understand the importance of meeting the emotional needs of the faculty and staff. Learn how to pay attention to your faculty and staff. Practice the art of listening with empathy and invest in coaching your faculty and staff. When a leader can coach from a position of interdependence and allow his or her faculty and staff to solve their own dilemmas, the leader builds capacity for the work at all levels.

f) *Designs and implements job-embedded and other opportunities for professional learning collaboratively with faculty and staff.*

Effective school leaders understand the importance of continuous learning for faculty and staff, and for self. Intentional planning for professional learning is necessary to sharpen each person's understanding of the common purpose of schooling and to support the mission, vision, and core values of the school.

Intentional design related to the data and what faculty and staff need is critical to school improvement. Each teacher should complete a professional growth plan, and the school leader needs to have multiple conversations related to long-term, job-embedded professional growth. Professional learning is no longer a one-time or one-day event but is related to the long-term development of faculty and staff. Have a plan and work the plan based on the strengths of your faculty and staff and the needs of your students. Ask the questions related to data, and what the data tell you, or doesn't tell you, about the professional growth of your faculty and staff.

Encourage faculty and staff to seek innovative instructional practices and then share them with all faculty and staff.

g) *Provides opportunities for collaborative examination of practice, collegial feedback, and collective learning.*

There is a wide variety of established protocols for teachers to analyze student work and make professional judgments based on the work. Effective leaders understand the importance of protecting scheduled time during the workday to allow faculty the opportunity to use protocols, examine student work samples, and offer suggestions to colleagues based on the work shared. Faculty develop stronger instructional strategies and ideas for improvement of pedagogy at all levels.

This transformative atmosphere is available when the leader understands the value of collaborative examination of work and intentionally schedules and plans for the structured learning processes based on the needs of the faculty and students.

h) *Encourages faculty-initiated improvement of programs and practices.*

Effective instructional leaders understand that a part of the job is to be the number one cheerleader for the faculty and staff. To be the encourager-in-chief sometimes means you encourage faculty to expand their learning by asking for volunteers for a research-based practice that needs to be piloted before expanding. Sometimes it is as simple as supporting a faculty-initiated idea or grant application. Plant seeds daily that will expand the learning of all faculty and staff. Encourage innovation and growth within teams, across grade levels or departments, and build collegiality in all settings. At the end of the day, we are all here to improve student learning at all levels.

SCENARIO

You could have heard a pin drop in the library when the superintendent finished speaking. The current principal was being replaced mid-year due to the continuing decline of state test scores. Two schools in the district failed to meet the state accountability mark, and both principals were being replaced by the end of the month. A district-selected interim principal would be assigned until a permanent administrator could be found. Miss Edwards sat quietly in the back of the room, waiting for the superintendent to introduce her as the interim. She heard her name, and took a deep breath, thinking, "Here we go."

Miss Edwards stepped forward and spoke quietly, "I understand this isn't a place you want to be for your students, but the data tells us we have work to do. Based on the information I have reviewed about your school, I believe we can develop a plan, make improvements, and work together by focusing on what is best for each child. I look forward to getting to know each of you and hope you will share your greatest dreams regarding your professional practice with our learning community."

Within the first month of the transition, the school had reviewed the school mission, vision, and core values, studied current student academic and nonacademic data, and developed a plan of improvement based on the most pressing problems related to student achievement. All faculty and staff reviewed the plan and established work groups to engage in the school's improvement.

One of the most important committees included the fifth-grade math teacher, Mrs. Marcum. The charge to the committee was to study the elementary schedule and develop a revised model for response to intervention. How could more time be provided during the day for teachers to meet collaboratively to study student work and plan instruction based on student needs? The committee had met multiple times and developed a couple of master schedule options for the school to review and adopt.

"Is there a specific time the committee can present the master schedule to the whole faculty?" Mrs. Marcum asked her new supervisor from the lunchroom doorway.

"Sure, we can add it to the Tuesday faculty agenda," replied Miss Edwards as she placed milk on student trays and guided them out into the cafeteria for lunch. "How do you feel about your options?"

Mrs. Marcum felt her team had done good work. "We reviewed multiple models, researched best times for instruction based on age, visited a couple of schools that are similar in make up to us, and reviewed our RtI processes. We think we are ready to share the recommendations with the faculty and staff."

"Great, let's make it happen," said Miss Edwards.

The following Tuesday, Mrs. Marcum shared the work of the committee. The teachers seemed to like the intentional focus on planning time related to grade-level teams.

"We can get so much work done related to enrichment and intervention," remarked one teacher.

"I can finally come watch how you teach that fraction lesson and follow up with questions," commented another.

"This is exciting!" replied a third teacher.

"What is the plan for communicating the new schedule to the parents?" asked Miss Edwards. "How will they know the schedules are changing and why?"

The faculty brainstormed ideas and shared with the committee. Next step communication plans were developed to share the new schedule with parents and the school community at large. The excitement related to the new student-focused master schedule was growing. Miss Edwards looked at the faculty sitting in the same library as a few months prior and reflected on the professional growth and collaborative work the group had shown. The work of developing professional learning communities within the school was moving in the right direction.

The Professional Community Leader:

- consistently monitors and evaluates working conditions and perceptions of the school by using perception data related to working conditions.
- collaboratively develops a plan to effectively affect professional development and student learning.
- communicates the data related to perceptions of school working conditions and related plans for improvement with all stakeholders.
- provides job-embedded structures for faculty/staff to learn from each other.
- intentionally designs professional learning experiences for faculty/staff based on data.
- celebrates successes of faculty/staff (both personal and professional).
- aligns all professional development for faculty/staff to school mission, vision, and core values.
- encourages faculty/staff to broaden learning and bring knew innovation and ideas to school community.
- intentionally schedules time for faculty/staff to study data, plan, and improve supports for student achievement.
- distributes leadership opportunities to faculty and staff to advance student learning and socio-emotional well-being.
- empowers faculty/staff to problem solve to meet the academic, social, emotional, and physical needs of each student and to support the school mission, vision, and core values.
- facilitates professional learning plan that aligns with growth goals of the school and supports the mission, vision, and core values of the school.
- models for school stakeholders in holding each other accountable for school improvement and in sharing responsibility for successes and failures (i.e., we are all in this together).
- communicates with data and shares school improvements widely.

- develops a culture of high trust.
- develops teacher expectation procedures.
- empowers and entrusts teachers to meet the academic, social, emotional, and physical needs of each student.
- supports open, caring, and professional relationships among faculty and staff.
- communicates and advocates for the needs and priorities of each student.
- ensures that all adopted strategies for student learning are grounded in research and best practice.

Questions for Further Reflection:

1) What did you learn about the importance of developing a collaborative professional community for faculty and staff? How will you use this new knowledge moving into the role of an instructional leader?
2) Why are investments in professional learning communities critical for the school's long-term effectiveness?
3) What intentional practices related to engaging diversity, innovation, and perspectives are currently practiced in your school? What practices can be added to increase collaborative professional practices?
4) How can protocols illuminate effective teaching practices and improve learning for all?
5) What are some ideas related to assessing and celebrating faculty/staff that might improve student achievement?
6) What additional skills or information do you need related to collaborative professional communities to continue your professional learning?

NOTE

1. Richard DuFour, Rebecca DuFour, Robert Eaker, and Thomas Many, *Learning by Doing: A Handbook for Professional Learning Communities at Work* Bloomington, IN: National Education Service, 2006.

Chapter 8

Meaningful Engagement of Families and Community

Debbie Powers

It takes a village to raise a child.

—African Proverb

Standard 8: Effective educational leaders engage families and the community in meaningful, reciprocal, and mutually beneficial ways to promote each student's academic success and well-being.

a) *Effective leaders are approachable, accessible, and welcoming to families and members of the community.*

Educational leaders are truly the ambassadors of their respective schools and districts. It is very much a "people business," and as such it is essential that school leaders both recognize and embrace that line of thinking. Gone are the days of school leaders sitting in their offices behind closed doors making important decisions. Our business requires us to interact with our community, both inside and outside of our respective buildings, in meaningful ways every single day.

How do we balance the demands of our professional instructional lives and managerial lives with the demands of engaging with families and the community? Well, you could work the carpool line. You could help check out student reading materials in the library. You could walk the sidelines at a soccer game or be present at a cheerleading event or an academic competition. What about hosting a community meeting at the school, such as the Lions Club?

71

Messaging is important, too. Is your phone greeting warm and personal? What about your "out of office" reply? Does it promote a feeling of accessibility? Do you schedule specific times in your day to return phone calls and emails? If you have a crisis and cannot do that in a timely fashion, have you developed the capacity in an assistant to do that on your behalf—simply letting people know you have not forgotten about them goes a long, long way with parents, caretakers, and community members.

Finally, take an environmental scan of your entry and office areas. Does the signage promote a positive and welcoming message for families and visitors? Is the waiting area free of clutter? Do you have a basket of books for younger children while they wait with their families or perhaps some small plastic toys to keep them amused? Maybe your office staff has a stash of crayons and coloring sheets available for younger siblings while they wait. Parents and caregivers would certainly appreciate that gesture. The tone you set goes beyond your personal interactions! Let your environment help you create that welcome feeling.

b) *Effective leaders create and sustain positive, collaborative, and productive relationships with families and the community for the benefit of students.*

"You never get a second chance to create a first impression," so the saying goes. Relationship building begins with the first eye contact with a new family, the first handshake, or the first greeting. That initial introduction sets the stage for all that is to follow. Sharing school success stories, promoting a feeling of pride in the school, and sharing a genuine "Welcome to our school!" greeting is essential, whether one on one or in a group setting.

Creating avenues to develop and sustain those positive, collaborative, and productive relationships will certainly serve you well in the times that are more challenging. When you take the time to invest in positive and collaborative relationships early, those efforts will come to serve you well at critical junctures. Budget shortfalls, program cutbacks, staffing issues, and building and maintenance issues can all cause strife for not only school leaders, but also the many and varied members of the school community. If you have previously established that all you do is for the benefit of the students, the community is more likely to rally to support the school, and you as the school leader, during those tough times.

Collaboration, however, is the key. Remember that in a collaborative relationship, all parties are benefitting from the collaboration. This is not a one-way street. Ensuring your families and the community feel both welcomed and valued as you work together to benefit the students should be the goal of creating and sustaining these important relationships.

c) *Engage in regular and open two-way communication with families and the community about the school, students, needs, problems, and accomplishments.*

Most schools have a weekly newsletter they distribute to parents and caregivers. Few extend that newsletter to community partners on a regular basis, which is something to consider, but weekly communication from the school is pretty routine. Social media platforms are relatively new to schools but still allow for regular information to be shared about events. Let's face it—these weekly newsletters and social media posts are mostly a way to share information updates and act as "good news forums" for parents, caretakers, and the community.

Helping schools develop the means to provide parents, caretakers, and community partners with viable avenues for two-way communication is difficult. The weekly newsletter and the social media postings are one-way communication strategies. Two-way communication requires both disseminating and receiving information. You cannot simply devise a survey to send out every time you want to solicit information, nor can you just put a suggestion box on the counter of the school office and hope people drop a note in there when they visit. Again, not an effective or viable means to promote two-way communication.

When looking to potentially difficult topics for discussion, such as deciding on a prioritized list of necessary expenditures or trying to reach consensus on which after-school programs are supported, or how to recognize both student scholars and student athletes in meaningful and timely ways, two-way communication is essential. Hosting forums for the community to not only learn about the issues but also to allow for important discussion is essential.

Information sessions with guided table-talk questions aimed at gathering input from parents, caretakers, and the community are effective means for nurturing two-way conversations. When school staff and the community engage in conversation, misunderstandings and misinformation are at a minimum. Relationships may be established, and new insights gained.

d) *Maintain a presence in the community to understand its strengths and needs, develop productive relationships, and engage its resources for the school.*

The school as an entity certainly maintains a presence in the community, but this item really is about the school leader maintaining a presence in the community. It is not enough to be present at the school events and athletic events in this day. You must find a way to interact and stay connected with community partners, including the business community. Yes, it is time consuming, but these interactions are important. It would be remiss to leave resources at the table unused, and you cannot make use of them if you do not know they exist!

If your community hosts events such as the Lions' Club or a small business association meeting, ask to attend. Offer to give a talk about your school activities or highlight the accomplishments of a student or two for the group. Find a way to network regularly with those community groups. Many of them offer scholarship dollars to students or could be open to internship opportunities, as well. Some may offer tuition assistance for employees, and your presence at these meetings is a terrific way to help connect students, parents, and caregivers to previously unknown resources in the community.

e) *Create means for the school community to partner with families to support student learning in and out of school.*

As the school leader, you are in a unique position to promote family and community engagement. The school, under your leadership, can become the conduit for information and services that support student learning between families and community programs and agencies. By maintaining a meaningful presence in the community, as noted previously, a school leader can then begin to help information flow to students and families through a new channel—the school communication system.

Many community organizations offer extended and summer learning opportunities for students. The school leader can make it possible to showcase those programs to students and families. School leaders should think about ways to increase parent and caregiver attendance at school events, and one way to do that is to "stack events" making it possible to include more than one group at a time. Some schools host an end-of-year art show. Consider combining that art show with a summer kick-off event that would allow organizations and programs to occupy information booths at that school-wide event. This would not only bring new people to the event but would also support local community groups by highlighting the school-community partnerships. This is just one example of capitalizing on school events to help establish and grow school-parent-community partnerships.

f) *Understand, value, and employ the community's cultural, social, intellectual, and political resources to promote student learning and school improvement.*

As you may know, there are many perspectives by which you must examine issues and occurrences to make the very best decision you can make on behalf of your school and your students. Schools often become the centerpiece of the community and as such represent all members of the community. Ensuring all stakeholder groups, and frankly subgroups of the stakeholder groups, have a voice at the school can be a daunting task. It is the combination of all facets of a school community that allows a rich tapestry to develop at the school reflective of the larger community.

You need to be sensitive to the scheduling of activities and events to avoid conflicts with other community events and activities that have long-standing traditions. Yes, you may have to work the annual Apple Festival into the life of the school each September because "that's what we do here" thinking is important for your school culture. You do not want to be the person to cancel that community event! Being a good citizen of the community, both as a school leader and as a school, entity is extremely important.

It is incumbent on school leaders to know their respective communities well. You must know the power brokers. You must know the service providers. You must know the unofficial caretakers of the community. You must know the history of relationships and how those past relationships will impact future work. In short, being aware of the multiple facets of the community and how those different parts work together—or not—will serve you well as a school leader.

g) *Develop and provide the school as a resource for families and the community.*

Effective school leaders certainly know how to advocate for their schools. Essential to that advocacy is to have already built meaningful relationships throughout the community. Certainly, it is possible to do that by establishing the school as a fundamental resource for both families and the community. It is not possible for a school to be a one-stop shop for parents and the community, but it is possible to be the conduit of information so that parents and the community see the school as both a critical partner and a valuable community resource.

The community makes substantial investments in the school in terms of financial support through tax monies and donations. Local businesses often support various programming and initiatives at the school, and one would be hard-pressed not to notice logos and signage of sponsorship on athletic fields and in gymnasiums. Effective school leaders recognize that local support is truly a two-way street; however, it is just as important to establish and develop as the two-way communication discussed earlier.

It is important for the school leader to embrace partnerships and to promote the school as a valuable resource to the community. Allowing outside groups to use the facility, with the appropriate legal precautions in place, is one way to demonstrate the school as a resource to the community. Another is to help sponsor programming at the school that may support community interests. For instance, offering a computer camp for parents and caregivers in the evenings or on a weekend may be a terrific way to help them overcome their fear of technology, allowing greater involvement by parents and caregivers in the school lives of their respective students. Making it known to local residential facilities that students and teachers are available to help socialize their residents through storytelling, art projects, music, or other activities can help the school gain valuable community exposure.

h) *Advocate for the school and district, and for the importance of education and student needs and priorities to families and the communities.*

Advocacy may be defined as garnering public support for a cause or policy of worth. It is essential for effective school leaders to learn to prioritize needs so that they may effectively advocate through all means to address those needs on behalf of the students—for the benefit of the community. Education has truly never been more important than it is now. The changing landscape of our global economy and the sweeping changes in our social systems are combining to create essentially a new world order. Mastering the use of technology as a tool is the key to this new order and without education as the driving force, communities may suffer economically. Education is the very lifeblood of progress today.

Beyond the simple definition mentioned above, advocacy may also be about supporting change. As our communities grow in complexity, schools and districts must find a way to grow with them. Long-term growth must be studied. The selling and buying of large parcels of land in a district may place an untold burden on a local school in three years with new homes, new families, and new students. Effective school leaders must stay cognizant of developments in the school community, and beyond, that may impact their districts and schools. They must help establish and promote the priorities of the schools and district in which they work to ensure community support.

To face facts, no one likes to talk about money, but districts regularly discuss the need for tax increase to support additional revenue requirements. While that action and decision lies at the district level, effective school leaders regularly communicate, in a two-way fashion, with their local communities highlighting the value of an education, the educational priorities of the school, and the means by which the school struggles to address those priorities. Through maintaining broad community awareness of and advocacy for local community needs, the discussion around something as difficult as a tax increase is far less contentious.

i) *Advocate publicly for the needs and priorities of students, and families, and the community.*

Previously, we mentioned the benefits of membership in groups like the Lions' Club and the small business associations in towns and counties. While important to help establish your personal presence in the community, active partnership with those groups provides the school leader a platform from which to advocate in positive and productive ways the priorities of the school, the families, and the students of the community. Highlighting both the positives at the school in terms of achievement and accomplishments, as well as the challenges such as programming or facility issues, will keep the community at large abreast of all facets of school life.

It is not enough to advocate within your community on behalf of the needs of your school; effective leaders must also assume a larger role of advocacy outside of their immediate school communities. Membership in state and national professional organizations provides not only essential information to practicing professionals but also allows a forum of advocacy for members. State committees and task forces allow school leaders to collaborate with others on behalf of common educational issues and priorities. National membership provides yet a broader audience for advocacy of educational priorities and goals. Effective school leaders seek out opportunities to advocate for their schools, their communities, and their students at every opportunity.

j) *Build and sustain productive partnerships with public and private sectors to promote school improvement and student learning.*

Relationships are the key to be an effective school leader. Trust, rapport, visibility, and accessibility have all been highlighted as essential traits for a school leader. Attending events and promoting the priorities of the school through speeches and newsletters are great ways to shine a light on the school in the short term, but it takes follow-up and persistence to sustain productive partnerships on behalf of your students. Visibility is important, but accessibility is essential.

Scheduling time for follow-up after events or even a phone call or email prior to an event is an excellent habit to develop. Those in leadership in the public and private sectors are busy professionals, and a courtesy email or phone call either with an invitation or a thank you lets them know that talking with you is both worth their time and valuable to you, as well. The personal outreach from one leader to another helps to strengthen a relationship that left unattended could merely be a formality rather than the beginning to a long-lasting, productive partnership.

SCENARIO

No one could have predicted the sudden economic downturn and the burden it placed on the community. Riverton is really no different from any small town in the United States, with an economy built on the shoulders of hard-working families. This economic downturn left families with one income where there had been two, and in some instances, two incomes to none. Life would be different for Riverton moving forward for the foreseeable future.

The school secretary first alerted me to one of the many impacts of the financial dilemma on our school when she told me about the calls inquiring about assistance. "Ms. Thomas, I have taken at least 15 calls today asking about sign-ups for the summer food program. I am not sure how to keep track of all the questions."

As the principal, I knew there would be impacts on our school from the economic crisis. With so many families now having at least one parent unemployed, I knew we would face requests for free and reduced lunch applications, field trip waivers, and the like. I also knew that as the spring fundraiser rolled around to support our 'arts' program, we would likely see the lowest amount of financial support in our history.

"Well, Miss Mays, let's just take the information from everyone calling and then we can take the issue to our planning team to discuss what we may need to do to support our students this summer." I tried not to appear worried.

Shifts had been cut back at the local industrial park as early as February. It was now the middle of April and the impact of the reductions was being felt across the county. I knew my school was not the only school facing these issues. I reached out to the district office and asked if we could discuss the summer food program, and the spring school and county events during our next leadership meeting. I explained that more schools than mine would be facing these issues and that perhaps together we could look for ways to address them. The superintendent agreed to put the items on the next meeting agenda.

Prior to our leadership meeting, I reached out to my fellow principals individually. I shared with each of them the increased interest in the summer food program as well as my concerns for not only our spring arts showcase fundraiser but also for all spring activities—many of which carried a hefty price tag. I learned about prom and graduation expenses for the high school, middle school spring sports costs, and our traditional elementary fundraisers for arts programs. We all agreed it may be best to band together at the district level to help address our common issues.

I talked with Miss Mays about the increase in requests for the summer food program, and I also asked her about the expenses related to the annual spring arts fundraiser—including what was normally expected as revenue from the event. I mean, the school secretary knows everything ...Or she knows how to find whatever it is you need. She told me there was a 200 percent increase in requests for participation in our summer food program (from 32 percent of our students previously to a whopping 96 percent of our students currently).

I just decided to round it up to 100 percent of our students needing food support for the summer. She also let me know that we annually would bring in over $3,000 from the arts showcase. That money was earmarked for supplies for our arts department to supplement the meager $150 allocation each of the two teachers received at the start of the school year.

I knew going into the district leadership meeting I was not the only principal facing such serious concerns. My colleagues had already shared many of their worries with me, and I had heard rumblings in the community as well. It was clear that a concerted, district-wide response to our issues would be the most effective and efficient way to help address what our schools were facing.

Mrs. Gamble, our superintendent, had already approached our local business community and our local civic organizations on behalf of the students and families in the district. Everyone was well aware of the dire situation developing across the county due to the layoffs and the subsequent blow to the local economy. She opened our meeting by thanking us and then invited each of us to share our immediate concerns with the group.

As each of the six principals shared their information, Mrs. Gamble was careful to record the main issues for each school on a poster and hung it on the wall. "Thank you for sharing your concerns with us. I am confident that with our collective efforts, we can address these issues. However, I know that with the collective efforts of the entire community, we will do a much better job of meeting the needs of our students and their families." And with that statement she let us know that she had invited members of the community to join us for a working lunch. Each principal would share the unique needs of their individual school and then, based on common themes and concerns, community members and school leaders would sit together at roundtables and discuss possible solutions.

All of the principals shared a look of surprise and delight. We knew we were not in this work alone, but for our superintendent to have already garnered community support for the students and our schools confirmed what we already knew about her. She had done a tremendous job of helping the community identify the schools as valuable and important contributing members of the community at large. As such, the community was willing to see the school as a resource for problem-solving and civic action.

These roundtable action groups were populated with a diverse mix of representatives. Civic leaders, business leaders, respected pastors and clergy, influential alumni, parents and grandparents all had been invited to be a part of the solution-seeking group. Every town in the district was represented by familiar faces to the principals—people with whom they had worked with and supported. It was an awesome experience for everyone.

I left that lunch meeting knowing that each of the action groups formed earlier would act with compassion, creativity, and commitment to ensure our students had a meaningful and memorable experience for all spring events, and that families and students would have adequate food for their summer meals. I was so excited to share with Miss Mays that the local hardware stores in each town in the county were going to help establish community gardens to help grow fresh produce for families.

The federal summer food program in which the district participated was extended to include all families in need, with expanded pickup locations and hours. The community churches would help support families on the weekends through their respective food pantries. The local craftsmen in the community had agreed to help support our students in turning their arts showcase into an internet event—able to reach people outside of the immediate area in the hope of meeting our annual sales goal. Like me, Miss Mays was shocked but delighted.

I went on to tell her the ladies auxiliary group was going to sponsor a Prom Day for the girls in the community, and would do hair and makeup at no cost—as well as collect gently used dresses to help offset the cost associated with the event. The Lion's Club agreed to sponsor food for the prom so that students would not have to try to scrape together money for a pre-prom dinner. The local sporting goods store, along with coaches and teams from the out of season sports, agreed to "adopt an athlete" at the middle school to ensure that every student interested in participating in spring sports would not be prevented from doing so due to expenses.

There was still much work to be done to ensure the needs of the community during this time of crisis would be addressed, but neither Miss Mays nor I could believe all that had been accomplished in a single meeting over lunch.

"Miss Mays, I am both amazed and delighted at how this community has come together to support our students and families." She smiled that knowing smile back at me that only school secretaries can pull off. She knew the community would rally and find a way.

"It's all about relationships," she said as she walked down the hallway. "It's all about relationships."

> *At the end of the day, the most overwhelming key to a child's success is the positive involvement of the parents. Jane D. Hull, Governor of Arizona 1997–2003*

Our greatest assets on behalf of the students populating our schools are their parents and caregivers. The roles they play in the lives of their children may help schools overcome perceived barriers. Those roles, if left unattended and unnurtured, may also become huge challenges for the school. Authentic relationships are absolutely essential.

In *Beyond the Bake Sale—The Essential Guide to School-Family Partnership,*[1] the authors note there are five basic roles parents play in school. They are as follows:

1. Parents as Partners-parents performing basic obligations for their child's education and social development.
2. Parents as Collaborators and Problem Solvers—parents reinforcing the school's efforts with their child and helping to solve problems.
3. Parents as Audience-parents attending and appreciating the school's and their child's performances and productions.
4. Parents as Supporters-parents providing volunteer assistance to teachers, the parent organization, and to other parents.
5. Parents as Advisors and/or Co-decision Makers-parents providing input on school policy and programs through membership in ad-hoc or permanent governance bodies.

Educators, especially school leaders, often struggle with a definition of authentic engagement for parents, caretakers, and the community. Authentic engagement should be meaningful. It should help move students forward academically, socially, and emotionally. The engagement should benefit students and in benefitting students, also benefit the school in meeting the needs of the students. Not every parent, not every family, not every community has the means by which to be full collaborators in the educational lives of their students.

Parents working a third shift would be hard-pressed to make an evening meeting or performance. Does that mean they do not care? Absolutely not! The grandmother of two elementary students having temporary custody of her grandchildren may only be able to get them dressed, fed, and on the bus every day due to her health or circumstance. Is she engaged? Yes. Can she do more? Likely not. Does she care any less about their safety and education? Of course not. She is authentically engaged with the school. Remember, we are not likely living in a world of two-parent families with easy access to mom or dad. Families look very different today and you must know your community, know your families, and know their capabilities as you work to ensure meaningful and authentic engagement. Your job is not to judge, your job is to engage.

Questions for Further Reflection:

1. What issues surrounding engaging parents, caregivers, and the community on behalf of students give you the most pause for thought as you begin the journey of school leadership?

2. Think back to a time when you were impressed with the actions of a school leader as they advocated for their school and their students. What traits and/or dispositions did that leader possess that caused them to be effective in the role of advocacy from your perspective?

3. What has been the best school-community partnership you have witnessed thus far in your career? What made it the best?

NOTE

1. Anne Henderson, Vivian Johnson, Karen Mapp, and Don Davies, *Beyond the Bake Sale: The Essential Guide to Family School Partnerships* USA: The New Press, 2007, 3.

Chapter 9

Operations and Management

Teresa Wallace

Management is about persuading people to do things they do not want to do, while leadership is about inspiring people to do things, they never thought they could.

—Steve Jobs

Standard 9: Effective educational leaders manage school operations and resources to promote each student's academic success and well-being.

With effective schools' research in the early 1980s, the focus of school principals moved from that of being a manager to that of being an instructional leader. However, the day-to-day operations of a school require the principal to complete many managerial tasks. The principal must be a leader at all times but must be a leader who manages well.

a) *Institute, manage, and monitor operations and administrative systems that promote the mission and vision of the schools.*

Research shows that the leader should involve various stakeholder groups in developing the mission and vision of the organization whether that be at the school- or district-level. Without an agreed-on purpose, the organization will not move forward. Once the mission and vision are developed, it is the responsibility of the leader, whether it be the principal at the school-level or the superintendent at the district-level, to ensure resources and structures are in place for the mission and vision to be achieved.

The leader must allocate, monitor, and manage resources and establish administrative systems that allow the mission and vision to be realized. At the same time the leader is managing to ensure the mission and vision are realized, he or she must be leading through collaboration with stakeholders, open communication, and shared decision-making. He/she cannot achieve the mission of the school or district alone.

(b) *Strategically manage staff resources, assigning and scheduling teachers and staff to roles and responsibilities that optimize their professional capacity to address each student's learning needs.*

Maya Angelou once said: "This is the value of the teacher, who looks at a face and says there's something behind that and I want to reach that person . . . . I want to call out that person who is behind that face, behind that color, behind that tradition, behind that culture. I believe you can do it. I know what was done for me."[1]

Only the teacher has a greater impact on student achievement than does the school principal. Therefore, it is imperative that the principal strategically manage human capital to optimize student learning. Sometimes, the best teachers are those teaching the highest-level students and doing the least amount of work in a building.

The principal must put the students, not the adults, first and assign teachers in a manner that optimizes their professional capacity and meets the learning needs of each student. It cannot be about which classes the teacher wants to teach. Instead, it must be about assigning the teacher to the class where he/she will be most effective in meeting the learning needs of students. Policies must be in place that allow the principal to make staff assignments based on areas of expertise and student needs.

c) *Seek, acquire, and manage fiscal, physical, and other resources to support curriculum, instruction, and assessment; student learning community; professional capacity and community; and family and community engagement.*

The school leader must continue to build upon the system of collaboration and shared decision-making implemented with stakeholders to establish the mission and vision of the school to acquire and manage resources. Leaders must strategically target all available resources to support increased student achievement. Acquiring resources often involves entities at the local, state, and national level. As resources are acquired from all levels, leaders must involve stakeholders at various levels in determining the allocation of those resources to support learning and build capacity at the family and community level.

Before leaders decide to apply for a grant or seek resources, he/she must ensure the allowed use of funds aligns with the learning goals and needs of the district. An abundance of resources does little to accomplish learning goals and meet district needs if the resources are not allowed to be used for these purposes. An example is funding for after-school programming for students, staff, or family members. Many times, this funding must be used after the close of the regular school day. The problem is many of the students needing the most assistance choose not to stay after school.

The same is true for teachers and family members. Teachers have completed their workday at a given time and many choose not to stay for professional learning after their contract day ends if they do not get paid for the extra time. Family members often have difficulty attending family gatherings after school because their little ones require them to be at home after the school day ends. The leader's time would be better spent searching and applying for resources that allow the programming during the school day.

d) *Are responsible, ethical, and accountable stewards of the school's monetary and nonmonetary resources, engaging in effective budgeting and accounting practices.*

It is not unusual to see stories in the newspaper about school leaders allowing resources to be stolen or used for purposes other than those intended. These incidents range from missing equipment to school employees stealing thousands of dollars, some of those raised by students. The first thought of many when reading the headlines is that the principal was irresponsible in managing the money and/ or resources. It is the responsibility of the principal to effectively manage and be a good steward of the school's resources. The principal must establish processes for collecting, depositing, budgeting, and spending all funds under his/her care.

The principal should require clubs, organizations, and anyone else raising funds using the school name to submit an annual budget. There should be an established process for recording and depositing all funds collected. Everyone involved should be clear on allowable expenditures from various funds.

The principal should have a designated employee who issues checks from any account, and purchase orders and invoices should be required for all checks written. All groups should submit an expenditure report at the end of the year for accountability purposes. Proper training should be provided to anyone involved in raising or expending money or resources on behalf of the school, and all accounts should be audited annually.

e) *Protect teachers' and other staff members' work and learning from disruption.*

School boards across the country have board policies outlining procedures to protect instructional time. They commonly state that it shall be the duty of the principal to ensure that other activities do not infringe upon instructional time. Schools often have policies specifying that intercom announcements must be made before or after the instructional day, and activities that reward or punish students must be conducted outside of instructional time. These policies typically specify that the principal will enforce the guidelines and will ensure that all staff are educated on the policy. Everyone is in agreement that the principal is responsible for protecting and monitoring instructional time to maximize student learning.

f) *Employ technology to improve the quality and efficiency of operations and management.*

Never before have school leaders had the resources at their fingertips that they have today. No longer are offices filled with filing cabinets and stacks of paper documents. Principals have the technology resources to improve the quality and efficiency of operations and management in a number of ways.

Parents or guardians of hundreds of students in a building can all receive the same message in a matter of minutes with software that allows the principal to make one phone call that goes out to all households. Teachers can receive immediate feedback from an observation or classroom walkthrough. Technology can be used to collect and analyze data in a fraction of the time it took only a few years ago. Principals can use technology to protect the school from data loss and to share data with numerous stakeholder groups. Administrative operations can become more efficient and effective, leaving the principal more time to focus on student achievement.

The effective school leader stays aware of trends and forecasts of data and technology in order to improve the efficiency of operations and management.

g) *Develop and maintain data and communication systems to deliver actionable information for classroom and school improvement.*

Principals must establish, monitor, and evaluate systems for collecting, analyzing, sharing, communicating, and using data to facilitate classroom and school improvement. It is the responsibility of the principal to establish a data-driven culture within the building and to provide ongoing data leadership. Teachers must become accustomed to using data to assess what students are learning and to determine what progress they are making toward their learning goals. Data must be used systematically to monitor school improvement.

The principal must provide a means, such as professional learning communities, for teachers to collaborate to analyze data and make instructional decisions to improve student, classroom, and school performance. The principal must also ensure teachers have the training and knowledge they need to use the data to ensure individual student needs are met.

A quote by Nat Turner, "Good communication is the bridge between confusion and clarity,"[2] supports the need for a principal to have a communication plan. The principal is constantly communicating with individuals and groups inside and outside the school building. He/she uses a range of formal and informal communication methods and skills daily. Although unplanned communication happens daily, the principal needs a communication plan to ensure proper stakeholder groups receive pertinent information. The plan should include the individuals or groups with whom the information will be shared, the reason for the communication, and the method of communicating.

Stakeholders, including faculty and staff, should have access to the communication plan, so they know which communication to expect, and when. For example, when state assessment data is released to the school, the principal should review the results with faculty and staff and prepare a report to submit to local media outlets and to post on social media at the earliest date permitted by the state. Having this in the communication plan informs parents when they may expect to have access to assessment data and reminds teachers that the principal will be the one to communicate this information to the community. The communication plan should be monitored and updated annually.

h) *Know, comply with, and help the school community understand local, state, and federal laws, rights, policies, and regulations so as to promote student success.*

The district has policies that govern operations within the district. These policies and accompanying procedures align with local, state, and federal laws and regulations and are available through the superintendent's office as public record for all stakeholders to review. From these policies, the principal should develop school-level policies that promote student success.

For example, at the federal level, the Every Student Succeeds Act of 2015 defines subgroups of students to be included when determining achievement gaps. At the state level in Kentucky, *KRS 158.649* directs the state department of education to provide, by October 1 of each year, state assessment data disaggregated by subgroup to each school. The related district policy outlines the process for distributing information on state assessments to schools. The school-level policy outlines the process for reviewing state assessment data and determining if achievement gap targets were met.

The principal must understand how local, state, and federal laws, policies, and regulations align to promote student success. He/she must then determine how the school, and the school-based decision-making council, if there is one, will align their policies and procedures to district-level policies and procedures. Policies and procedures should be reviewed regularly and revised as necessary. The process for informing stakeholders of revisions should be included in the school communication plan.

i) *Develop and manage relationships with feeder and connecting schools for enrollment management and curricular and instructional articulation.*

Whether in a large or small district, there never seems to be enough time to adequately address vertical curriculum and instruction issues. This requires effort on the part of the leadership at both the feeder and connecting schools. It would be ideal if teachers from all elementary feeder schools could meet together with teachers in the middle school regularly to align curriculum and discuss effective instructional strategies for specific students, or even groups of students, but it is a struggle to make this happen. The principal must reach out to the principals of the feeder schools and build relationships conducive to data sharing and collaboration.

At minimum, the principal should arrange for the teachers to meet by department each summer to discuss the incoming students and share any information the middle school teachers need to know before the students arrive. The principal should work with the feeder school principals to schedule common staff meetings for the teachers to work on vertical curriculum alignment at any time standards or instructional programs change.

j) *Develop and manage productive relationships with the central office and school board.*

If a principal wants to be successful in a district, he/she must work at building productive relationships with the central office, especially the superintendent. The principal does not have to agree with the superintendent at all times, but there must be an understanding of how that disagreement will be shared and with whom. No superintendent wants a principal criticizing him/her in public. On the other hand, the principal must have the support of the superintendent, especially with personnel-related issues. In many states, the teachers are employees of the board and must be hired, disciplined, and terminated by the superintendent. The principal must work closely with the superintendent to resolve personnel issues within the school building.

The relationship between the principal and school board members should be productive simply because parents and other community members often take their complaints about administrators to board members. The principal needs to have the trust of the board member, so he or she will refer the person to the superintendent to discuss personnel issues instead of sharing his or her opinion on the issue. The superintendent evaluates principal performance and should be the one to hear complaints related to performance.

k) *Develop and administer systems for fair and equitable management of conflict among students, faculty and staff, leaders, families, and community.*

The principal must work collaboratively with stakeholders to develop systems for fairly and equitably managing conflict among various groups. There needs to be a plan of how to deal with conflict before conflict arises, and the principal needs to have the authority to administer the plan. A student handbook that includes conflict resolution processes should be developed with input from students, faculty, staff, other administrators, parents/guardians, and community representatives. The student handbook should be shared with all stakeholder groups at the beginning of each school year. The principal should follow the processes outlined in the handbook when resolving conflict to ensure consistent, fair, and equitable management of conflict and to let all stakeholders know the plan is being followed.

The principal should also have a faculty and staff handbook developed with inputs from faculty, staff, and the district human resource office. Conflict resolution policies and procedures should be included and should be implemented as written when conflict arises. Consistent, fair, and equitable conflict management is again paramount when dealing with faculty and staff conflict.

The school should have policies that are implemented by the principal to manage conflict that may arise with families and communities. Families and community members should be aware of the policies, and they should be followed when working to resolve conflict. The principal should strive to create a culture where stakeholders take responsibility for managing the conflict, but he or she should have processes to rely on when conflict does occur.

l) *Manage governance processes and internal and external politics toward achieving the school's mission and vision.*

No principal or school leader can avoid politics in education. What one must do is keep the focus on the school's mission and vision and improving student achievement. If the principal keeps the attitude of always doing what is best for students at the forefront, it is difficult for politicians or anyone else to say he/she is wrong.

SCENARIO

Karen was concerned over what she was seeing in how her veteran principal, Mr. Reilly, was handling the school. This was her third year as his assistant principal, and she had learned the processes and procedures of proper school management while attending school district leadership team meetings. She felt she needed to ask Ms. Hemlepp, the school secretary, if she was noticing the same carelessness.

"Peggy let's chat. I need to ask you something . . . . Is Mr. Reilly on top of things as he used to be?"

Ms. Hemlepp had served the school as office manager for twenty years. Everyone in the county knew "Peggy." She was a matriarch in the community and as competent and honest as the day is long. She looked away for a moment, and then began to cry.

> I don't know what has happened to him, Karen. He was supposed to retire two years ago, then his son lost his job. I think his family needs him to keep working in a big way, but I've noticed it too. He used to be on top of everything in this building—but not anymore. I'm not sure he even knows, or cares, much these days about how the funds are spent, how the custodians are doing their work, or how the evening activities are being monitored.

Peggy reached for a Kleenex.

> I have wanted to warn him to be more careful, but I don't know how to . . .This school is like a zoo. People are ordering supplies without a purchasing order . . . . He says "yes" to every vendor who walks in here. . . . The PTA and Athletic Boosters aren't following state guidelines for how to track their activity accounts . . . . Meetings with parents are cancelled on short notice for no reason . . . . The student discipline that he used to be known for has deteriorated to the point it's embarrassing to have visitors in the building.

"Ok. That's all I needed to know. You don't worry about it anymore—I'll talk to him. I have an idea." Karen needed an evening just to think and clear her head but scheduled an hour with her boss for early the next morning, just after the AM announcements.

"Hey, Sir. Brought you some donuts. Have been thinking a lot lately about how much I still need to learn before I sit in the hot seat someday. Who knows, may not be at this school. But there's going to come a time when I'll be asked to take my turn being the lead principal somewhere."

"Why Karen, I sure hope it's here. You have been a wonderful assistant principal, and we don't know what we would do without you around here."

"Thank you, Sir. But I think I fall short a lot. What I really need is more experience in all of the management stuff. You do that, and I run the instructional part pretty well. But, with our new curriculum coach being assigned here by the district office, I wonder if you'd let me learn the ropes on what you do. I'd be honored to oversee the operations part of the job, and let you mentor me."

Mr. Reilly looked a bit shocked but kept his always gentle persona in front of any mixed feelings he was having at the moment. "Well, that's not a bad plan, young lady. But what would I do—after I've shown you the ins and outs?"

"Well Sir, what if you enjoy during your time left in this job what you've earned after almost thirty years of leading and serving schools."

"And how would I do that Karen? What do you mean?"

Well, if I take on the management stuff, then what if you spent most of your time doing what I've heard has made you a legend in this town? Spend a lot of time every day simply chatting with people. Have lunch with students. Visit with faculty on their planning block. Go to Rotary to represent the school. Go on field trips again. Enjoy a game every now and then. Have some coffee with old Joe and get him cleaning this school the right way again . . .

Mr. Reilly sat back in his chair, looked wistfully out the window of his office, wiped a tear from his eye and nodded. "I'd like that Karen. I'd like that very much . . . . Maybe I still have a bit left in me—like I used to. Just need to pass the reins on to you and do what I used to be so good at—caring for people . . . . Maybe I should retire this summer . . . . But, let's try this and see how it works."

"Let's do it Sir!"

Karen walked out in the hallway and down to her office. And she too wept quietly, but in a good way—knowing she had done a noble thing, and with the heart of a servant leader.

The Managerial Leader:

• nurtures a respectful relationship with students, families, staff, teachers, central office administrators, superintendent, school board members, and community.

- becomes familiar with the district board policies and procedures.
- always keeps the focus on what's best for students.
- collaboratively develops student and staff/faculty handbooks and adheres to them.
- listens respectfully to parents, staff, students, and other stakeholders when conflict arises.
- manages to ensure the mission and vision of the school are realized.
- strategically manages human capital to optimize student learning. (i.e., always puts the student first).
- serves as a responsible, ethical, and accountable steward of the school's monetary and nonmonetary resources.
- protects and monitors instructional time to maximize student learning.
- utilizes technology to improve the quality and efficiency of operations and management.
- keeps refining communication skills and methods of communicating with various stakeholder groups.
- participates in workshops and attends conferences to stay current on state and federal laws and regulations.
- gets to know other principals in the district (i.e., will need their assistance with feeder and receiver school issues).
- does not get caught up in local, state, or national politics (i.e., will lose focus on what is best for students).

And, remember the words of Condoleezza Rice: "Every good leader is part manager and every good manager is part leader."[3] You cannot avoid the managerial duties as a school leader.

Questions for Further Reflection:

1. What systems and processes do you need to put in place to ensure you manage school operations and resources to promote the academic success and well-being of every student in your building?
2. Who do you know that you can call on when you have questions about school operations and management issues?
3. How will you always keep the focus on doing what is best for your students?

NOTES

1. Pamela Tucker and James H. Stronge, "Linking Teacher Evaluation and Student Learning," ASCD, 2005, 1.

2. Retrieved from https://www.quotetab.com/.

3. Retrieved from https://www.azquotes.com/.

Chapter 10

School Improvement

Stephanie Sullivan

School improvement depends on principals who can foster the conditions necessary for sustained education reform in a complex, rapidly-changing society. Never has the time been riper for change leaders than now.

—Michael Fullan

Standard 10: Effective educational leaders act as agents of continuous improvement to promote each student's academic success and well-being.

a) *Seek to make school more effective for each student, teachers and staff, families, and the community.*

While traveling, one nomad asked the other, "Are we there yet?" The other nomad replied, "Of course not, we are nomads." Much like nomads, effective leaders should never be completely satisfied that they have reached a destination. In a rapidly, ever-changing environment, a school leader must be continually evaluating the system to determine areas in which the organization can improve. The role of an effective school leader is not one of complacency, but one more indicative of a nomad–one seeking where to go next on the journey to success as milestones are reached and goals are accomplished.

As a new principal, it is easy to think: "Wow, things will be a lot easier next year once I learn what it is I am supposed to be doing." However, the reality is that it never really gets easier. The more school leaders learn, the more they are aware of the many ways the organization can be improved.

They soon realize there is so much to be done that the ability to make improvements cannot be accomplished on their own. The effective leader must empower those around him or her to help achieve the school's mission.

Whether placed in the highest performing school in a district, or the lowest performing school, there are always areas that can be improved. And, there are so many areas to consider—culture, academics, communication, engagement, discipline, personnel, mentoring, professional development, data analysis, community outreach, and the list goes on and on. So, it is important to prioritize and tackle those that are deemed most important. Take that first step toward that first goal, and once it's reached, let the momentum of its success continue to drive future endeavors.

So, "Are we there yet?" may be a mindset of a mediocre leader, but an effective leader is a nomad—Constantly seeking the next path to making the school more effective for students, teachers and staff, families, and the community.

b) *Use methods of continuous improvement to achieve the vision, fulfill the mission, and promote the core values of the school.*

Often educators may become frustrated thinking the finish line is continually moving. Just when the school seems to be making progress and goals are within reach, new reform efforts are implemented, and a higher bar is set. The effective school leader must set the example for keeping high expectations that adhere to the vision, mission, and core values of the school. It is important not to get caught in a trap of negativity by saying things like "This is just the next new thing," "This too shall pass," or "Just wait long enough, and it will all cycle back around."

If the principal models this type of negative attitude, it will spread throughout the entire school. As new expectations, standards, and challenges are presented, the leader should find ways to connect them to the school's vision. When stakeholders believe in an initiative and see that its purpose aligns to the school's ideals, they will more likely be committed to its success. With dedication comes hard work, and with hard work comes success.

There must be a process to monitor and prioritize continuous improvement efforts. Should this be accomplished solely by the principal? No. Effective school leaders must include stakeholders to develop a school-wide commitment. A needs assessment should be conducted by stakeholders to help determine *where we are* and *where we want to be* by creating measurable and accomplishable goals. Through strategic planning, goals should be established, and a detailed plan of action should be created, communicated, implemented, monitored, revised, and evaluated.

The Comprehensive School Improvement Plan (CSIP), which is required by the state, addresses the academic needs of a school; however, other plans may be created to target other types of needs. These plans may be derived from collaboration with groups such as the Parent Teacher Organization (PTO), students, staff, or the community. Improvement plans may be as simple as enhancing the playground with new equipment or as complex as utilizing the business sector to provide internships to prepare students for work after graduation.

When plans are being created, keep in mind that there is not always a need to reinvent the wheel. Take advantage of pioneers in the field who have already paved the way in the area you have targeted for improvement. Learn from their successes and failures to create a plan that best fits your organization.

c) *Prepare the school and the community for improvement, promoting readiness, an imperative for improvement, instilling mutual commitment and accountability, and developing the knowledge, skills, and motivation to succeed in improvement.*

One key ingredient to preparing the school for improvement is communication. All steps of the improvement plan will be enhanced with effective communication. Communicate the needs, communicate the goal, communicate the plan, communicate the progress, communicate the results, and communicate the success. When communicating often and with transparency, it builds trust that, in turn, promotes buy-in and commitment from stakeholders to all phases of the improvement plan.

To motivate the school to succeed in improvement efforts requires a culture that seeks to continually improve. It takes true dedication to give the time, commitment, and energy toward doing whatever it takes to make the school the best it can be for its students, staff, and community. The leader must be the example and display dedication to making difficult decisions—the decisions that do not necessarily make things easier, but those that make things better for all involved. Doing what is needed is not always an easy task.

As the leader sets the tone for striving toward excellence, others need to be provided a voice and an opportunity for input. As staff, parents, community, and students are empowered, it instills a sense of ownership and pride that is a catalyst for hard work and commitment. As stakeholders become involved, it may be necessary to provide additional training, resources, and/or support to effectively engage them in professional dialogue and action, which will lead to making situationally appropriate decisions for school improvement.

Effective leaders must be the example for exhibiting true commitment and passion to endeavors that promote student success and well-being by creating a change culture, where members are willing and optimistic to make real-time changes as needed to positively impact students and the school.

d) *Engage others in an ongoing process of evidence-based inquiry, learning, strategic goal setting, planning, implementation, and evaluation for continuous school and classroom improvement.*

Who should be involved on a school improvement team? As school improvement teams are developed, it is important to have diverse perspectives. Although it may seem easier to designate school improvement committee members that will not "ruffle any feathers" and will simply "go with the flow," having limited perspectives is not the best way to have true school improvement. Even if everything goes smoothly at first, once the plan is implemented, problems may arise that could have been alleviated in the planning stage if diverse perspectives had been allowed.

An effective school leader must have an open mind and not get trapped in the traditional mindset of "That's the way we've always done it." Leaders must be open to new and innovative approaches that may be introduced. Committee membership should include those who will provide diverse perspectives, as well as those who will be most impacted by the decisions.

Once the team is created, how will you ensure all voices are heard? It may be important to create norms upon which the team can agree. As opinions are shared, all decisions may not reach a consensus. It will be important for the school leader to create an environment in which the team can "agree to disagree" at times, while still working toward the unified goal of school improvement. Is there a time to take a stand? Is there a time to yield? Will compromises have to be made for the greater good? How will the school leader navigate the good, bad, and ugly of getting people to work together and share diverse ideas in a positive way that unifies the team?

Once data has been used to identify and prioritize needs, goals must be created. When developing goals, they should be measurable. The data provides a starting point, and the team must agree on what is going to be achieved and when. How will the goal be measured? What formative/summative data will be gathered? When should this goal be attained?

While the CSIP provides the platform to create measurable academic goals, don't forget that these same rules should apply to other school improvement efforts. What data do you have to justify the identified school need? Were surveys conducted? Was a climate survey used? Did students vote? Did the PTO members provide suggestions or feedback?

To ensure all necessary components are included, a Specific, Measurable, Achievable, Realistic, and Timely (SMART) goal can be created. When determining the specific components, one must consider the 5 W's—Who, What, When, Where and Why.[1] Once the goal is established, it is necessary to create a strategic plan of action. There are many steps that must take place, with multiple people involved, for school improvement efforts to be successful.

While students may think a playground magically appears over the weekend, many people have been involved in the process. A few of those steps may have included submitting a letter for approval to the board of education, organizing fund-raising efforts, researching the safest and most cost-effective equipment to purchase, and coordinating with the district maintenance department to ensure installation is completed according to code. Who will be responsible for each of these steps? That must be outlined in the plan, along with a timeline to ensure the project stays on track.

Once the plan of action is determined, the real work begins. While many people may be involved, the school leader must ensure everyone is doing their part during each phase of implementation and adhering to the timeline. During implementation, it is important to have various checkpoints, where the committee reconvenes to monitor the progress. It may be necessary to revise the plan if new information is presented, or adequate progress is not being made.

At the conclusion of implementation, data once again must be collected to evaluate goal attainment. If the goal was reached, then that success needs to be communicated and celebrated. Some goals may reach completion, while others may be ongoing, resulting in continual refinement and implementation.

For example, a short-term goal, such as installing new playground equipment, may not need further refinement. Everyone can celebrate the successful attainment of new equipment; however, a long-term goal, such as increasing the number of students reaching proficiency in fifth-grade writing, may involve refinement and a continuation of implementation the following year. While a small, measurable goal may have been reached, the goal may now be enhanced with additional training for more teachers to expand the plan to the primary grades for a new specific, measurable, attainable, realistic goal that adheres to timelines.

At each stage of the school improvement plan, two things are important to keep at the forefront—communication and data. Both are important in the stages of needs identification, goal setting, implementation, monitoring, refinement and evaluation.

e) *Employ situationally appropriate strategies for improvement, including transformational and incremental, adaptive approaches and attention to different phases of implementation.*

How do you eat an elephant? One bite at a time. It is certainly okay to set lofty goals; however, they may need to be balanced with incremental goals. It may not be attainable or realistic to go from 20 percent proficiency to 80 percent proficiency in reading in one school year, but with incremental goals, a school can reach success. Timelines for monitoring must be defined, with checkpoints for incremental goals. As those goals are reached, celebrate that success. Success is a huge motivator. It fuels the drive to continue pushing toward the goal. Before long, what once seemed unattainable is now within reach.

f) *Assess and develop the capacity of staff to assess the value and applicability of emerging educational trends and the findings of research for the school and its improvement.*

When a new initiative is presented to the staff, such as providing a "Stop Everything and Read" time during the school schedule, has the research been shared on why this is a best practice for improving reading achievement? If the school leader requests a school-wide technology program to be purchased with SBDM instructional funds, has the research been shared on the product's effectiveness and how often the resource must be used to expect the anticipated academic gains?

An effective leader expects teachers to be proactive in staying abreast of current research. For example, before a teacher makes a request to group his or her students by ability, he or she should already be familiar with what the research says regarding ability grouping. Using research to make important school improvement decisions will result in greater confidence in end results. Decisions made on facts, instead of opinions, are more likely to lead to success rather than wasting time and energy on unsuccessful efforts.

One way that leaders can develop the capacity of their staff to access current trends and research in education is to lead book studies, facilitate professional learning, and share current instructional information regularly through professional learning communities and other staff communication. As a school leader, it is important to know the latest educational research and to engage the staff in those conversations. There are so many things to be done in a school that it may seem impossible to get everything accomplished, but by applying research-based practices, a school will operate more efficiently and effectively by working smarter, not harder.

Educators join this profession to make a difference in the lives of children, so the desire to help students is at the heart of every teacher. Teachers think they cannot possibly work any harder, and that is probably true, but often what is being done may not be producing the greatest gains. So, to make the biggest impact on a child, know the research and make sure all the energy being exerted each day is dedicated to those practices which have been proven to make a difference.

g) *Develop technically appropriate systems of data collection, management, analysis, and use, connecting as needed to the district office and external partners for support in planning, implementation, monitoring, feedback, and evaluation.*

DATA—That word can make the difference in a school being a "Needs Improvement" school, 4-Star school, or even a Blue-Ribbon School of Excellence. Without using data to drive instruction, it is almost impossible to monitor if appropriate growth is being made, or which standards have been mastered. Each student is different. Students develop academically at different stages, and they have been exposed to different life experiences that have impacted their learning. It is the responsibility of the teacher to regularly monitor data to make appropriate instructional decisions, and it is the effective school leader's responsibility to provide the means to collect, manage, analyze, and use that data to drive instruction throughout the school.

Once the school has identified a formative assessment tool for progress monitoring, the school leader must set in place the process for leading teachers to effectively use the data. This may involve creating a specific time each week/month that allows teachers to analyze the data. The effective school leader should model the use of reports to make instructional decisions which may include making schedule changes, creating opportunities for co-teaching, encouraging classroom peer observations, purchasing additional resources, and providing additional training for staff.

h) *Adopt a systems perspective and promote coherence among improvement efforts and all aspects of school organization, programs, and services.*

The effective school leader must create a system that supports improvement efforts. Academically, that can be accomplished by scheduling regular Professional Learning Community (PLC) meetings to analyze data and make informed instructional decisions, creating an agenda for each meeting to ensure the conversations stay focused on the goal, and modeling/leading an instructional data meeting. Data notebooks, data walls, or other data systems should be organized and consistent throughout the school. While various grade-level or content-area meetings are held, all need to be focused on predetermined objectives.

Nonacademic data may also be important toward a school's improvement efforts. The number of volunteers in a school may be impactful for a reading project; community engagement may be important to make students more aware of career choices; and attendance rates may be a predictor of student achievement. When working on these types of goals, external partners and other support staff may be beneficial to include on a school improvement committee, such as the Family Resource Center staff, business partners, civic organizations, and churches. As with academic meetings, there should always be an agenda with an objective to be accomplished. Meetings should also be scheduled at a time convenient for all members of the committee to be present.

i) *Manage uncertainty, risk, competing initiatives, and politics of change with courage and perseverance, providing support and encouragement, and openly communicating the need for, process for, and outcomes of improvement efforts.*

Can more than one school improvement effort be implemented? Yes. Can the principal be the sole leader and micro-manager of every step of the process for all initiatives? No. An effective school leader can oversee multiple initiatives by empowering others who have the skills to successfully lead. School improvement plans can be highly complex with multiple layers of implementation, while others can be simplistic and achieved within a relatively short amount of time.

For example, having a goal of increasing the percentage of students performing at the proficient level on writing on-demand may involve stages of professional development, multi-grade vertical alignment, and a school-wide writing plan including observation, coaching, tuning protocol, common assessments, and progress monitoring. This plan will extend throughout the entire school year, and may require additional refinement to continue throughout future years.

On the other hand, less complex improvement plans may include creating a safer and more efficient way of dismissing students or revising school behavior management plans. Regardless of the change, always be sure to communicate the new expectations and monitor the plan to ensure objectives are achieved.

It may seem like a daunting task to facilitate the creation, enforcement, evaluation, and refinement of all these plans; however, the effective school leader empowers others to be instrumental in school improvement efforts. A department chair or instructional coach may lead the writing initiative, a lead teacher may organize the student dismissal procedures, and an assistant principal may revamp the behavior system. Although others have been empowered to take the lead on specific plans, it is important that the school leader stays in close communication with the chairs of these committees and shows support for each. Without the message from the school leader that the improvement effort is important, it will soon lose momentum and end without success.

j) *Develop and promote leadership among teachers and staff for inquiry, experimentation and innovation, and initiating and implementing improvement.*

Beyond empowering others to take the lead in improvement efforts, are others provided the opportunity to freely express areas in which they feel improvements should be made? In what ways are voices allowed to be heard? What steps are taken to encourage others to identify areas that may need to be improved? Are only teachers provided that input? Are parents included? Do students have a voice? Do you allow staff to take risks as they try innovative approaches? Is there a regular survey of strengths and areas for growth for the school, or do improvement efforts get implemented only after problems surface?

The effective school leader must be proactive to combat problems before they occur by promoting a culture of change. "Are we there yet?" may only apply to a milestone on a journey of school improvement. We must continually strive to promote student success and well-being in this ever-changing environment.

SCENARIO

Pam had been a principal for the past three years and was now thrilled to be named as the first principal to the newly established elementary school in the district. Excitement could be felt everywhere. Teachers were anxious for a new start in a new school; students were excited as they were making new friends; and parents were eager to get involved. While the school board had made many of the decisions such as the school design, wall colors, and flooring, there were still some important things to determine—such as the mascot. Letters were sent to all students who were assigned to the school through redistricting, allowing each person to submit their vote for the school mascot. This helped create a sense of ownership and belonging as a contributing voice to the school.

Parents who had been active in their child's/children's previous school were eager to stay involved. Since the school did not have items such as trophy cases, scoreboards, speaker systems, or even textbooks, the parent organization, in collaboration with the school principal and secretary, began planning fund-raising events—which included a Summer Bash that allowed parents and students to meet their teachers and tour the new school. It was an exciting time!

Principal Pam wanted to take advantage of this commitment to seeing the school be successful, so a team was formed to be proactive and put procedures, activities, and events in place that would help define the school. The committee meeting was advertised, and there was such a tremendous turnout there was not an empty seat in the school library. It was standing room only. The principal welcomed those in attendance and shared her vision for the school. She explained that she was eager to hear others' expectations and what they envisioned for their child/children. She explained that the ideas generated from this meeting would help define the school. Parents openly and eagerly shared ideas for family events and celebrations for students. Many parent volunteered to donate their time and/or money to fulfill some needs that had not yet been met. The meeting was a great success, and many events were planned that would become traditions for years to come.

There was now a lot of work to be done. Pam knew that it would be important for future involvement that parents, teachers, and students knew their ideas were heard. As procedures were established and events planned, progress was shared in a monthly newsletter. Support was strong and momentum continued to grow.

Principal Pam stayed in close communication with the PTO, and met with the officers each month to create an agenda before the actual PTO meeting. This allowed for productive communication and collaboration to accomplish many goals for the school, including the determination of how funds would be spent. Following the Summer Bash, the PTO sent out a survey to parents asking them to identify and rank the needs of the school. These results were communicated in a newsletter and discussed at the monthly meeting. Using this input, the PTO prioritized its wish list, from popcorn machines to playground equipment to stage curtains. This communication encouraged families to donate items that were not able to be included in the budget.

At the end of the year, Principal Pam was very pleased with the progress that had been made that first year. She greatly valued the support and collaboration of the staff and the PTO organization. With their assistance, many items had been purchased that would not have been possible otherwise. Reflecting on the year, Pam pondered how this same excitement could be generated the following year. She knew this was a golden opportunity, and she realized it was important to continue this supportive partnership.

Principal Pam decided to create a school improvement committee that consisted of grade-level representation and met with this team and the PTO officers to discuss the school improvement efforts for the past year. The group determined which goals were met and which goals needed refinement. They decided to communicate with the students and their families by sending home a newsletter, thanking them for their help in making the inaugural year such a great success. Space for comments was provided to encourage parents and students to share what they would like to see accomplished in the upcoming year.

The team set a date to meet to review the comments received from the end of the year newsletter. Based on those results, a new improvement plan would be created for the upcoming school year.

Effective Change Agent Leaders:

- use data to drive decisions.
- involve stakeholders.
- prioritize needs.
- create measurable goals.
- implement a detailed plan, including timelines and the people responsible.
- monitor progress regularly.
- revise plans as needed.
- evaluate and refine goals.
- celebrate success.
- Communicate—communicate—communicate!

Questions for Further Reflection:

1. Based on the above scenario, what aspects of an effective school improvement plan were or were not evident?
2. Consider a time that your organization implemented a school improvement effort. What contributed to its success or failure? In what ways could it have been improved?
3. In what ways have school improvement efforts led to innovation?

Thinking Toward the Future:

4. How will you determine your school/district needs?
5. What data will drive your decisions?
6. Who will you include on your school improvement team?
7. In what ways will you communicate, and with whom?

NOTE

1. Corporate Finance Institute (2015–2020). Retrieved from https://corporatefinanceinstitute.com/resources/knowledge/other/smart-goal/.

Chapter 11

Kentucky's Implementation of PSEL

Jenny Ray and Stacy Noah

Our goals can only be reached through a vehicle of a plan, in which we must fervently believe, and upon which we must vigorously act. There is no other route to success.

—Pablo Picasso

IMPLEMENTATION MATTERS

The Professional Standards for Educational Leaders (PSEL) are the required standards for principals and assistant principals. Thus, the "what" has already been determined for Kentucky educators. The exciting part of this process is that the "how" is open and encouraged for districts and or schools to develop. *How* the leadership standards are used is in the hands of those implementing the standards.

COMPLIANCE VS. COMMITMENT

PSEL is a mandated component of the school leaders' required evaluation system in Kentucky. Notice the word "required." There is no opt-out of PSEL or evaluation, *but* there is a choice regarding the type of implementation that occurs and the resulting outcome. Compliance implementation will allow for all the i's to be dotted and the t's to be crossed and that is essential when dealing with a regulatory requirement. It is important to follow the rules and policies to the letter of the law. Compliance is not a bad aspect of evaluation implementation; however, it should not be the end goal of implementation.

Instead, moving beyond compliance to commitment is the lever to promote meaningful implementation of standards that results in the highest levels of principal quality.

Without question, the end goal is grounded in Kentucky's commitment to every school being led by an effective leader as part of a continuous cycle of improvement. So, what does effective mean? How does one know what effective looks like in practice? What ensures "effective" has the same meaning for all?

Fortunately, effective practice is qualified by the PSEL. The standards articulate the leadership that Kentucky schools need, and students deserve. They are student-centric, outlining foundational principles of leadership to guide the practice of educational leaders, so they can move the needle on student learning and achieve more equitable outcomes. They are designed to ensure that educational leaders are ready to meet challenges of the job today and in the future as education, schools and society continue to transform.

With this description, it is obvious that the depth of the standards is immense. As each of the ten standards has numerous elements that provide additional clarity and meaning, deep understanding is paramount to the successful implementation of an evaluation system that embodies commitment by all.

Consequently, the Kentucky Department of Education (KDE), specifically the Office of Educator Licensure and Effectiveness (OELE), has partnered with numerous educational entities to develop resources and tools to support a deep understanding and readiness for PSEL implementation as part of a growth-oriented evaluation system. Facilitated by KDE's Principal Partnership Project (P3), modules and accompanying resources have been created to equip users with not only foundational knowledge but also implementation strategies and supports that highlight collaborative coaching models designed to catalyze professional growth and effectiveness.

Additionally, Kentucky principals, superintendents, University Principal Preparation Initiative (UPPI), cooperative representatives, and KDE Leadership constructed the KY PSEL Growth and Evaluation Tool. The Tool is a valuable resource that schools and/or districts can personalize to connect with essential needs and priorities. Kentucky-designed components of the Tool are four performance levels with correlated progressive language, critical attributes, and possible examples designed to promote district calibration and affirm implementation expectations for PSEL. While the resources and supports referenced are most helpful, just having them does not guarantee movement from compliance to commitment.

For example, Principal A completes the PSEL professional learning modules in one sitting primarily because a set amount of professional development hours is required to be completed by a certain date. Principal B, with passionate enthusiasm, encourages fellow leaders to complete the modules and schedules time periodically to reflect together on the content. Principal B advocates the value of the professional learning series as a springboard to promote self-growth, leadership effectiveness, and continuous improvement of overall job performance. Which principal is compliant and which principal is committed? Which principal do you want to be? Which principal do you want leading your child's school?

Undoubtedly, Principal B's actions indicate commitment. Actions reflect being *all in* and focused on achieving stellar results instead of "just going through the motions" and meeting the minimum requirements. While it sounds simple enough, building commitment is not easy. There is no magic wand that can be waved and "poof" there is commitment. However, with focused energy, leaders can inspire others to be internally motivated and in turn, *committed*.

What is necessary to build commitment to a highly effective evaluation system using PSEL as the criteria for success? Many factors feed into inspiring commitment, but leaders must be especially cognizant of the following motivators: culture, calibration, and conceptualization.

CULTURE

To ensure a principal evaluation system provokes growth and improvement, a culture committed to those attributes must be intentionally nurtured. The principal supervisor must constantly stoke the values by modeling growth mindset behaviors and utilizing supportive leadership-coaching strategies targeted to maximize performance. Just as an effective teacher develops a purpose statement/learning objective with students, district leadership's first step is to work collaboratively to detail the purpose of the evaluation system and intended use of the PSEL.

Identifying the district's core convictions of the system goes a long way in creating the intended culture. Notice the idea of working collaboratively. A critical step in building commitment is building ownership. Working together (evaluator and evaluatee, district teams) in determining the core convictions of the system make all parties developers of the system. Ownership is automatic, and in turn, meaning and purpose are instilled in all. Leaders are setting the stage for implementation in this initial work by capitalizing on the individual team members to create a group agreement around purpose and vision of the system. Critical to this foundational development is the application of the commitment to purpose. It is imperative the principal supervisor "walks the talk."

How might the culture of commitment be impacted if the principal supervisor's actions do not align with the consensus agreement of the system's purpose? What might be the impact on culture when this misalignment occurs?

Examine the following scenario. District leadership collaboratively developed core convictions of the Principal Evaluation System which included a high value on growth and improvement and coaching as a strategy to support agreed-upon priorities. During a conference after a site visit, the principal supervisor begins the meeting by saying to the principal, "You must do a better job at communicating with parents. I am getting all kinds of complaints about parents not knowing what's going on at the school." Definitely, two-way communication with parents is a vital leadership expectation that deserves attention.

However, the type of attention that is given is significant in this scenario. By immediately jumping into consulting, the principal supervisor abandoned the district's conviction of *coaching* for improvement, which likely resulted in an unintended consequence of depleting trust in the system and the supervisor. This, in turn, negatively impacted the desired culture of commitment and instead, likely, bred a survival mode mentality in the principal.

Perhaps this scenario may have ended differently if the principal supervisor had instead asked a series of coaching questions such as (1) What feedback have you received from parents regarding the school's communication efforts? (2) What additional communication routes might you consider in order to continue to strive to reach more parents? (3) Thinking about what is most important for students' families to know and understand, what do you do to ensure that information is effectively communicated to them?

This coaching stance frames the questions with two positive presuppositions: the principal is aware that communication with parents is an issue, and he/she is striving to do better. Coaching questions, because they are framed with genuine inquiry instead of accusation, allow for more honest reflection and response. Equally as important, the district's convictions were modeled by the principal supervisor, fostering a culture of trust.

The culture of your environment will influence your ability to coach. Likewise, actions reflect culture. You make a choice every single time you respond. By dominating a conversation, that choice is based less on the other person and more on you. To support a culture that values the process of others coming to their own understanding, people at the top must model action that reflects the collective beliefs and values that in turn influence policies and practices in the district.

CALIBRATION

"Getting on the same page" is a strategy to build commitment. Using the same language is one thing but internalizing the meaning of the language the same way as others is reaching a much deeper commitment level. For example, in the PSEL there is language that resonates meaning and provides guidance on high-quality leadership. Thus, it is imperative that district teams "get on the same page" regarding the PSEL. An effective process to support mutual meaning is the use of a protocol to facilitate deep learning and strengthen the evaluation system.

Focusing on critical language and embedded skills and dispositions, district teams can find monumental value in deconstructing the PSEL as a means to calibrate meaning and expectation. Using an analytical perspective, district teams can instill commitment to the same interpretation and expectation of leadership effectiveness. A close examination of Standard 6, *Element a* illustrates the power of using a protocol to ensure group consensus. *Figure 11.1* shows the protocol.

Thinking critically about *Element a* brings to life the depth of this one element and verifies the importance of district calibration to support commitment. Doing a close read of *Element a*, consider the following questions: How do you interpret this element? What are important words embedded in this element? What can you conclude initially about this element?

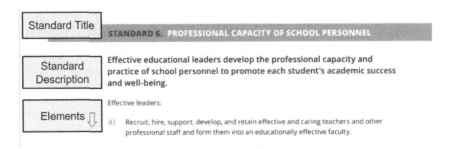

Standard Title	STANDARD 6. PROFESSIONAL CAPACITY OF SCHOOL PERSONNEL
Standard Description	Effective educational leaders develop the professional capacity and practice of school personnel to promote each student's academic success and well-being.
Elements ⇩	Effective leaders: a) Recruit, hire, support, develop, and retain effective and caring teachers and other professional staff and form them into an educationally effective faculty.

Figure 11.1.   Protocol for Deconstructing PSEL Standards.

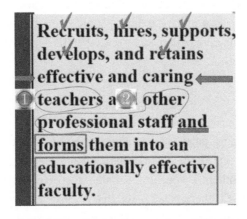

Figure 11.2.   Illustration of Close Read and Annotation of the Element.

Now, let's do a second read of the element. Silently re-read the goal language and think even more critically about the text.

Now that you have had your think time, let's make meaning of this element. We will do a close read of this element's text and use an annotation strategy to support an analytical breakdown of the element. *Figure 11.2* illustrates the close read and annotation of the element.

To begin, the opening text clues us in to five essential actions: recruits, hires, supports, develops, and retains. So, the school leader is responsible for those specific actions. Now the question is, recruit, hire, support, develop, and retain WHO?

There are two groups referenced in the element: Teachers and Other Professional Staff. As well, there is clarity given as to characteristics of these two groups. Qualifying descriptions are provided. The Teachers and Other Professional Staff must be EFFECTIVE and CARING.

Then, a close examination of the text draws our attention to the word AND. In addition to recruiting, hiring, supporting, developing and retaining effective and caring teachers and other professional staff, the connecting word AND indicates there is an additional layer of expectation embedded into this element.

The school leader is also expected to FORM the two identified groups into an educationally effective faculty. Clearly, the secondary layer of expectation increases the depth and complexity of this element. There is a critical lift identified when the school leader has the responsibility of creating a culture of collective efficacy that embraces a team mentality instead of isolated individuals working diligently behind closed classroom doors.

In thinking about the knowledge and skills needed for one to master this element's expectation, it is quite extensive. There is a specific reference to ensuring teachers and other professional staff are effective and caring. A closer inspection of the word EFFECTIVE magnifies necessary knowledge and skills. Consider these questions as you reflect on this vital word. What knowledge might a school leader need to ensure the two groups explicitly referenced are *effective*? How might having a strong handle on the criteria for success, for these two groups, be especially useful for the school leader? How might strategies utilized be different for each independent group?

Upon review, it is apparent that an accomplished school leader must have expertise in the role-specific criteria and be masterfully equipped with a skill set that inspires group members to be intrinsically motivated to grow and improve. Clearly, complex leadership expectations are ingrained within the text of the element.

Another significant knowledge requirement is strategies. To support attainment of this goal, knowing intentional and impactful strategies to support the action required in this element will be a positive addition to the leader's skill set. For instance, purposeful strategies targeted to support recruitment efforts would be a core knowledge expectation for this element.

In terms of skill, what skills might a school leader need to possess in order to perform at the Accomplished level? Certainly, the skill of collaboration is one of the primary competencies embedded in this element. To form independent groups into an educationally effective faculty, will require masterful collaboration skills. Having stellar collaboration skills will assist in the building of a culture designed to increase collective teacher efficacy while possibly utilizing teacher leadership as a lever.

As the team mentality is highlighted in this element, a team approach is also crucial to enhance leadership practices for all school leaders in the district. Working as a team, by facilitating calibrating conversations that create unity in meaning and application of standards, is a pivotal method to support leadership growth and ensure school and student success while also building commitment.

CONCEPTUALIZATION

Just as knowledge and skills enhance a school leader's understanding of details associated with each responsibility an accomplished leader is charged with executing, a conceptualized view of the standard is vital for improving practice and building commitment. A way to internalize a standard element is to bring it to life. Thus, a question to consider is: What might this look like in practice?

Through an extensive review of *Element a* meaning and expectation are clear. An important next step is to connect *Element a* to authentic examples of leadership practice to support conceptualization. The element mandates the school leader focuses on retention efforts.

How might evidence be captured to verify a focus on retention is resulting in positive outcomes? One such way is the use of a Stay Survey that is given to faculty to gauge why the employees stay and what could trigger them to leave. According to this accomplished possible example from the KY PSEL Guidance for Growth and Evaluation Tool, it is not just administering a Stay Survey, but it also requires analyzing the results to inform improved retention efforts. It is not simply about using a survey. It is much deeper than simple usage. There is correlated action in response to feedback. *Figure 11.3* shows the stay survey evidence example.

> *Stay Survey* **results are analyzed to inform retention efforts and feedback guides decisions regarding retention efforts.**

Figure 11.3.   Evidence Example—Stay Survey.

A second possible example connects to the embedded requirement of effectiveness. How might a school leader increase levels of effectiveness in teachers and other professional staff? One such way is to use a focused process such as the Danielson Collaborative Observation Process to support growth and improvement of all. Certainly, this process is not the only process a school could use. The difference-maker is having an identified process that is research-based and works for the specific school/district. *Figure 11.4* illustrates this second evidence example.

Lastly is a possible example that references some specific peer observation strategies like Pineapple Charts and #observe me. These are specific activities, if implemented with fidelity, which the school leader facilitates to build an accountable, collaborative culture for growth and improvement. As such, the element's end goal is the creation of an educationally effective faculty. To bring individual teachers together, teachers are the key ingredient. If done well, peer observation strategies promote partnerships and collegial connections that contribute to the fruition of a faculty, a collective group sharing mutual accountability, a team. *Figure 11.5* provides the evidence of this example.

For additional possible examples to prompt thinking regarding the conceptualization of specific leadership practices, access to the KY PSEL Guidance

> **With fidelity, the school uses Danielson's Collaborative Observation Process as a tool to support growth.**

Figure 11.4.   Evidence Example Danielson's Observation Process.

> **Peer feedback initiatives, like Pineapple Charts & #ObserveMe, are visibly supported and prioritized by school leadership.**

Figure 11.5.   Peer Observation Strategies.

for Growth and Effectiveness Tool is provided here: https://sites.google.com/ education.ky.gov/principalpartnership/psel-modules.

Locate the Possible Examples Section in the Tool to Review.

In closing, years of research have confirmed the gravity of both teacher quality and school leadership relative to improved student achievement. While teacher quality is the single biggest factor influencing student achievement, strong principals are paramount to teacher development and retention. In fact, principals account for 25 percent—and teachers 33 percent—of a school's total impact on student achievement. As leadership is such an influential component nurturing school and student success, prioritization of quality leadership development, that requires coaching and reflection as the primary driver, is a decisive act to support a culture of unceasing growth and improvement.

Therefore, investment in the continuous development of principal practice is a hallmark of a district's and/or school's improvement efforts. District commitment to a high-quality principal evaluation system, aimed at improving professional effectiveness and maximizing performance as it relates to PSEL implementation, is essential to promoting meaningful change that is proudly evidenced by improved teaching and learning.

Moreover, developing a shared understanding of standards and rubrics, providing consistent professional learning support to calibrate raters and their interpretations of a standard related to any given performance, and prioritizing the development of skilled evaluators are essential attributes to the development of a quality evaluation system. Principals deserve nothing less. As the WHAT is clear, the next step is HOW.

At the beginning of this chapter, the opening statement was *Implementation Matters*. Validating the importance of the implementation process, *HOW* will your district implement PSEL? What implementation plan might be developed to best support the skill development of learning-focused school leaders? How might your district empower principals to grow and improve while also precisely adhering to statutory requirements? There is no single "recipe" for success when it comes to implementation, but there is the single ingredient of enduring commitment to mutually agreed-upon expectations for growth and improvement that can certainly enhance district systems and routines for elevating principal support.

Implementation Discussion Questions for Districts

1. As you examine your district's PSEL Professional Learning Plan, what strategies/supports might be most helpful to promote change and encourage continuous improvement?

2. In terms of PSEL implementation readiness, how ready is your district? What evidence validates readiness level?

3. How might your district ensure the regulatory requirement of evaluation does not become a checklist grounded in compliance but instead seizes the mandate as a lever to propel meaningful implementation of standards that promotes a culture of continuous improvement?

4. What might be the benefit of the principal supervisor fully engaging in PSEL professional learning and dialogue with principals? What might be an unintended consequence if the principal supervisor does not learn alongside principals?

5. While some may view new standards as a challenge, how might your district send the message that new standards are opportunities to get better?

Reflection Questions

1. The shift in thinking about evaluation from a *gotcha* system to a *growth-focused* system is pivotal in improving professional effectiveness and maximizing performance as it relates to a defined set of standards. Recognizing the necessity of a growth-focused evaluation system for principals, what steps need to be taken to affirm actions that reflect commitment to the attributes of a growth-focused system?
   - As a principal supervisor, how might you advocate and validate a growth-focused evaluation system for principals/assistant principals?
   - As a principal being evaluated, how might you be a leader among leaders to advocate the value of a growth-focused system with action?
   - As a principal charged with evaluating teachers, how might you improve the teacher evaluation system you facilitate to emulate the attributes of a growth-focused system?

2. Think about implementation efforts that you have been a part of during your career either as a teacher or principal.
   - Which one truly resulted in change and lasting impact? How do you know? What were the defining characteristics?

- Which one would you label a failure? Why? What were the defining characteristics?
- What did you learn from each (both effective and ineffective implementation efforts) that might positively inform the implementation plan of the PSEL and evaluation system?
- How might you use your experience regarding effective and ineffective implementation efforts to advocate for the most meaningful implementation of the PSEL and evaluation?
- What specific aspects of effective implementation practices might you find most useful to interject into the teacher evaluation system you facilitate?

3. Specifically clarifying the consensus purpose of the principal evaluation system and implementation of the PSEL are pivotal onboarding steps to support success.
   - How might you promulgate the necessity of jointly constructing purpose and implementation plans with intermittent checks for success?
   - How might neglecting the noted onboarding steps impact culture, commitment, and conceptualization?
   - As an evaluator of teachers, how effective have you been in facilitating the development of consensus purpose and correlated action steps for the teacher evaluation system? How do you know? What might be your indicators of success? What might be your next steps?

Chapter 12

Closing Thoughts

Greg Goins

It has generally been my experience that the very top people of truly great organizations are servant-leaders.

—Stephen Covey

SCENARIO

As a middle school principal, Kyle had to wear many different hats as the lone administrator in the building. Among his various duties was night-time supervision of home basketball games that included crowd control, supervising workers, and providing oversight for gate and concession receipts. With a booming voice, he also volunteered to be the public address announcer, making general announcements and introducing the starting line-ups.

One particular night, the school's athletic director (AD) walked up behind Kyle and said, "Hey, we're in a bind tonight. One of the officials just called and said he can't make it. Any ideas?"

With time winding down before tip-off, finding an official at the last minute was going to be next to impossible. It was at that moment that Kyle, a former college player and high school coach, jumped into action—finding a pair of tennis shoes to match his black dress pants and exchanging his necktie for a whistle.

With both coaches agreeing to use a substitute official, Kyle selected a student leader from the crowd to handle the announcing duties, the AD offered to help with crowd control, and the school secretary—who had a son on the team—agreed to handle the change box for the night. In the blink of an eye, everyone was "all in" as the home team split a pair, losing the JV game before rolling to a big victory in the varsity contest without a single controversial call by the officials.

After the game, Kyle quickly returned to principal mode—turning off lights, locking doors, and cleaning up from a busy night. That's when Tom, the night-time custodian, looked over at Kyle and said, "You know, I've worked in this school for almost 20 years now, and I've never had a principal like you."

With a sly grin, Kyle said, "What do you mean?"

Tom said, "Well first of all, I've never had a principal help me clean up after ball games or stay late to help take out the trash. Most principals don't want to get their hands dirty. And now I've seen everything—the school principal shows up in a tie and leaves in a striped (referee) shirt. My wife will never believe this story."

After sharing a laugh in the hallway, Kyle said, "Let me tell you a little secret Tom. It says *'principal'* in big bold letters on my office door, and sometimes that intimidates people when they have to come see me. But the last thing we need in this world right now is more conflict and division. I want to build relationships with people, especially our parents and students, so everyone understands that we're all in this together. For me, it's all about servant leadership."

Before Tom could say a word, Kyle looked him in the eye and said, "You know Tom, I probably don't say this enough, but you're a big part of this school, and I appreciate all you do to make this a special place. Be sure to tell your wife I said hello, and that I hope to see her soon."

As Tom returned to sweeping the gym floor, he broke into a smile as he watched his principal climb to the top of the bleachers to close an open window. "Yep," he thought. "We're all in this together."

In the above scenario, Kyle is a perfect example of the type of leadership we need in our schools today. Not because he saved the day as a substitute official, but because he understands that leadership, more than anything else, is a transfer of belief and a collaborative process that includes everyone, not just the person in the big office. The *secret* that Kyle shared above is that the very best leaders always *serve* others and lift people up, creating a positive culture built around trust, hope, and infinite possibilities for the future.

Throughout this book, various experts in the field of educational leadership have provided a clear blueprint on how to use PSEL in your role as a school principal. But to reach your full potential as a school leader, it's imperative that you recognize why the word student is used a total of fifty-three times throughout PSEL's ten standards and eighty-three elements, more than any other word throughout the document—providing clear guidance that creating student-centered schools is the overarching goal for all school leaders. By comparison, words such as *manage* and *evaluate* are used sparingly, only to reinforce necessary job duties.

Simply put, if the words *serve* and *student* are at the forefront of effective leadership, then shouldn't all decisions be made based on what's in the best interest of kids?

If you're looking for more evidence that servant leadership breaks the mold of traditional management and supervision, look no further than University of Kentucky men's basketball coach, John Calipari, who has led the Wildcats to four Final Fours and the 2012 NCAA men's championship over a ten-year period, entering the Naismith Basketball Hall of Fame in 2015.

For all of his success on the court, Calipari's impact as a servant leader off the court has been even more impressive as he's raised millions of dollars through the Calipari Foundation, created in 2012 to "enrich the lives of children." Through his service work, Calipari has raised millions of dollars in the aftermath of natural disasters, including the earthquake in Haiti (2010), Superstorm Sandy (2012), and Hurricane Harvey (2017). In 2019, Calipari and his wife, Ellen, also assisted federal workers with financial help during the government shutdown.

Most recently, the Calipari Foundation joined forces with Kroger in 2020 to provide meals to needy families in Fayette County Public Schools after school closures due to the Covid-19 pandemic. In addition, Calipari, always a champion for social justice, started a new Executive Development Program for minorities in the University of Kentucky Athletic Department in the wake of nation-wide protests of racial inequality.

Known as a "Players First" Coach, Calipari is driven by his own personal responsibility to develop individual players, both on and off the court, which ultimately brings a stronger work ethic and greater accountability to team success on the court. That mentality is also the driving force behind Calipari's focus on equity and cultural responsiveness as he's able to "ensure that each student has equitable access to effective teachers, learning opportunities, academic and social support, and other resources necessary for success" (PSEL 3C) and "alter institutional biases of student marginalization, deficit-based schooling, and low expectations associated with race, class, culture and language, gender and sexual orientation, and disability or special status" (PSEL 3E).

Regarding leadership, Calipari makes the following statement:

> Effective leadership starts with serving others. It's about making whatever you're doing about others. We call it servant leadership. It's not about you as a leader; it's about the people you are serving. You can't lead others if they don't know you're for them and for their interests and needs. If the people you're leading don't feel like you're one of them, that you're on the ground fighting for them, you'll never effectively lead. I tell our players all the time, you can't expect to be the leader of the team if you're not in there with your teammates battling with them every day. You can't lead from the sidelines. You've got to be in it with them. And then part of it is sacrificing and understanding how to share and how to give in to the greater good of the team. I would just say make it about others. Everyone faces daily pressures and tough decisions that weigh us down. Make it about the kids. If every decision they make is about helping their kids grow and succeed, everything else will take care of itself.

One of Calipari's favorite stories about personal sacrifice comes from the 2012 national title game, when Kentucky beat Kansas 67-59 in New Orleans to win its eighth national championship.

"You've probably heard me tell this story before, but Anthony Davis took the fifth most shots on our team," said Calipari. Didn't affect his ability to lead one bit. He was the National Player of the Year, the No. 1 pick in the draft, and the MVP of the national championship game. In that game, he made one shot. He couldn't make a thing. He told his teammates at halftime, "I can't make anything, so you all take all the shots. I'll grab every rebound and block every shot." He missed tip-ins, jump shots, dunks. And he was still the MVP. He told his teammates, 'I don't need to shoot the ball; you all do that and let's win'. It wasn't about numbers with him.

For Calipari, success on the basketball court, just like in our schools, comes from building trust and embracing a culture of togetherness and team building. That's why he typically begins each new season with a team book study that has included among others, *The Energy Bus: 10 Rules to Fuel Your Life, Work, and Team with Positive Energy*, written by best-selling author Jon Gordon, a world renown speaker on positive leadership.

"What makes him (Coach Calipari) special is the way he develops relationships with his players," said Gordon, who has worked with numerous college and professional sports teams including the Los Angeles Dodgers, Atlanta Falcons, and Miami Heat. "They know he really cares about them and loves them. It's not an act. That's who he really is."

Just twelve miles up the road from Kentucky's historic Rupp Arena is the campus of Georgetown College, founded in 1829, with its own legacy of academic and athletic success—offering a championship-level education of the heart and mind.

Georgetown College, once the training campsite for the NFL's Cincinnati Bengals, has a proud tradition in football, winning its first NAIA National Championship in 1991, and back-to-back titles in 2000 and 2001 under Head Coach Bill Cronin, who was inducted into the NAIA Hall of Fame in 2019. The men's basketball program is also a three-time national champion, most recently winning the 2019 title.

Among Georgetown's most notable alumni is Woodford County, Kentucky native Chris Hogan, a two-time No. 1 best-selling author, personal finance expert, and popular speaker and podcast host with Ramsey Solutions, a Nashville, Tennessee company created by Dave Ramsey, a financial guru and popular radio personality.

Hogan, a 1994 graduate of Georgetown College, was an All-American football player and key member of the Tigers first national championship team in 1991. That experience, coupled with his past as a one-time financial advisor to professional athletes and celebrities, has made Hogan a popular speaker on leadership, team building, and positive culture.

For Hogan, the key to effective leadership is simply having a keen awareness of your own personal ethics and professional norms as outlined in PSEL 2B that encourages leaders to "act according to and promote the professional norms of integrity, fairness, transparency, trust, collaboration, perseverance, learning, and continuous improvement."

"I've had an opportunity to be around some incredibly successful entrepreneurs, some incredibly successful leaders and one of the things that they do, there are a few things that really jump out at me, but number one, they're humble, which means that it's not about them," said Hogan, the author of *Everyday Millionaires: How Ordinary People Built Extraordinary Wealth— and How You Can Too,* and *Retire* and *Inspired: It's Not an Age; It's a Financial Number.* "They understand that it's about the team or their product or service that they represent, but they also take responsibility, which means if something didn't go well or something didn't work, they own it. But they're also looking for a solution and so that just has impressed me so much, in a culture that doesn't tend to do that, so it really sticks out like a sore thumb."

The big question is what does it mean to be a servant leader in your role as a school principal, or more importantly, how can PSEL guide you to become more intentional in how you interact with school and community stakeholders?

According to Larry Spears[1], former president of the Robert K. Greenleaf Center for Servant Leadership, there are ten characteristics of servant leadership. Each one is defined below with the applicable PSEL standard to serve as your own guide for implementation.

1. **Listening**—PSEL 8c: Engage in regular and open two-way communication with families and the community about the school, students, needs, problems, and accomplishments.

The first step to becoming a servant leader is in becoming a better listener. Too many times, school leaders get caught up in the day-to-day chaos and simply don't take the time to stop, listen, and reflect on conversations with adults and children. Sometimes, it's not about problem-solving, it's simply offering support so others can be heard.

2. **Empathy**—PSEL 2c: Lead with interpersonal and communication skill, social-emotional insight, and understanding of all students' and staff members' backgrounds and cultures.

Understand that everyone has their own unique, authentic perspective based on past experiences. As a school leader, you must always have an open mind and value other opinions.

3. **Healing**—PSEL 6h: Promote the personal and professional health, well-being, and work-life balance of faculty and staff.

Few things are as stressful as working in the field of education as schools have become a one-stop-shop for wellness, offering emotional support and wrap around services that includes everything from coat drives to packing weekend lunches. Don't forget your own health as putting others first does not mean that you can neglect your own spiritual growth and work-life balance.

4. **Awareness**—PSEL 2a: Act ethically and professionally in personal conduct, relationships with others, decision-making, stewardship of the school's resources, and all aspects of school leadership.

Perhaps the greatest challenge in serving as a school leader is in handling your own emotions, as there are many highs and lows that come with the job. It's important to start every day with a clean slate, providing a smile and high fives to those you lead. Your attitude and body language both play a pivotal role in the culture of your building.

5. **Persuasion**—PSEL10i: Manage uncertainty, risk, competing initiatives, and politics of change with courage and perseverance, providing support and encouragement, and openly communicating the need for, process for, and outcomes of improvement efforts.

At some point, others will look to you for courage in making tough decisions. However, this process must include collaborative efforts within your school and community to assure that all voices are part of the discussion. Remember, persuasion is not about manipulating others or a slick sales pitch. It's about building consensus around big ideas and finding a shared path to school improvement.

6. **Conceptualization**—PSEL7c: Establish and sustain a professional culture of engagement and commitment to shared vision, goals, and objectives pertaining to the education of the whole child; high expectations for professional work; ethical and equitable practice; trust and open communication; collaboration, collective efficacy, and continuous individual and organizational learning and improvement.

The very best school leaders have the innate ability to dream big and "think outside the box" when it comes to defining school success. To be more direct, visionary leadership is about having the courage to find new solutions to old problems and then holding firm in your belief that new, innovative strategies will take your school to the next level.

7. **Foresight**—PSEL 10d: Engage others in an ongoing process of evidence-based inquiry, learning, strategic goal setting, planning, implementation, and evaluation for continuous school and classroom improvement.

In an ever-changing world of disruptive technology, school leaders must have the ability to see into the future, understanding the conditions for change that are necessary to prepare students for the future. As such, school leaders must always be engaged in strategic planning to maintain a long-term vision for better schools.

8. **Stewardship**—PSEL3c: Confront and alter institutional biases of student marginalization, deficit-based schooling, and low expectations associated with race, class, culture and language, gender and sexual orientation, and disability or special status.

At first glance, one might think that stewardship is simply about managing financial resources. However, in this case, that's just one part of servant leadership as school leaders must also take responsibility—top to bottom—for everything that happens in our schools. Leaders must have a moral compass that models desired behaviors and expectations for sustained success.

9. **Commitment to the Growth of People**—PSEL 6c: Develop teachers' and staff members' professional knowledge, skills, and practice through differentiated opportunities for learning and growth, guided by understanding of professional and adult learning and development.

As school leaders, we must create a culture of innovation and risk taking that allows others to grow both personally and professionally. Provide teachers with relevant and meaningful professional learning opportunities that provide choice in their own learning.

10. **Building Community**—PSEL 1b: In collaboration with members of the school and the community and using relevant data, develop and promote

a vision for the school on the successful learning and development of each child and on instructional and organizational practices that promote such success.

Nothing is more important than building a community of trust, excitement, and a common purpose within organizations. School leaders must create a culture that values a team approach that is both student-centered and one that builds positive school and community relations.

If you put all ten characteristics together collectively, you'll most certainly find yourself thinking differently about the impact you can make as a school principal. In fact, Gordon, author of *The Power of Positive Leadership: How and Why Positive Leaders Transform Teams and Organizations and Change the World,* closes with a subtle reminder as to the impact great leaders can have on school districts.

Most importantly, Gordon understands that leaders must have a clear mission, vision and core values as outlined in PSEL 1C to help "articulate, advocate, and cultivate core values that define the school's culture and stress the imperative of child-centered education; high expectations and student support; equity, inclusiveness, and social justice; openness, caring, and trust; and continuous improvement."

"We will ultimately transform our school system by bringing great leaders into every school," said Gordon, co-founder of The Energy Bus for Schools Leadership Journey, a multi-year training program on creating positive school culture. "You bring a great principal into that school. That principal will transform that school just as a coach will transform a football program. You have a great leader, you have a great superintendent who cares about the kids, cares about the schools, you will transform that school. So my goal is that if we can develop great leaders and positive leaders in every single school in America, we will transform our education system."

Questions for Further Reflection:

1. Can you think of examples in your own school where someone has made personal sacrifices for the good of the team? Do you have an Anthony Davis in your school?
2. How can you become more intentional about your own self-awareness as a positive school leader? Could leading your own book study on

positivity and team building be a vehicle to create more servant leaders in your school?

3. Of the ten characteristics of servant leadership described in this chapter, which ones might be a priority for you in your own personal growth as a school leader?

NOTE

1. Larry Spears, "Character and Servant Leadership: Ten Characteristics of Effective, Caring Leaders," *The Journal of Virtues & Leadership* 1 (2010): 5–30.

Afterword

Standard One of the Professional Standards for Educational Leaders is:

"Effective educational leaders develop, advocate, and enact a shared vision and core values of high-quality education and academic success and well-being of each student."

From the perspective of a former school leader now working in the educator preparation space, *School Leadership: Let Professional Standards for Educational Leaders (PSEL) Make Your Work More Effective* is an exemplary review of what leader preparation can look like when a truly shared vision is developed by all stakeholders.

As a former high school principal, I often felt the disconnect between the theory taught in the preparation programs and the reality of working in the field. This book bridges that gap and provides a model that should become the gold standard for the development of all educator preparation programs.

In addition, it provides "real-world" guidance for school practitioners based on the work of local school leaders and leader educators.

I hope that as you study the lessons learned and takeaways from this text you will find the tools and inspiration to make PSEL work for you.

Rob Akers
Associate Commissioner
Office of Educator Licensure and Effectiveness
Kentucky Department of Education

Bibliography

Blum, Robert W. "A Case for School Connectedness." *Educational Leadership* 62, no. 7 (2005): 16–20.

Calipari, John. September 23, 2018. Email interview.

Carolus, John. Retrieved from https://www.activityvillage.co.uk/teacher-quotes.

CASEL. "What is Social and Emotional Learning?" Retrieved from https://school-guide.casel.org/what-is-sel/what-is-sel/.

Center on PBIS. "What is PBIS?" Retrieved from https://www.pbis.org.

Clifford, Matthew, Ellen Sherrat, and Jenni Fetters. *The Ripple Effect: A Synthesis of Research on Principal Influence to Inform Performance Evaluation Design.* Washington, DC: American Institutes for Research, 2012.

Corporate Finance Institute, 2015-2020. Retrieved from https://corporatefinanceinstitute.com/resources/knowledge/other/smart-goal/.

Darling-Hammond, Linda, and Channa Cook-Harvey. *Educating the Whole Child: Improving School Climate to Support Students.* Palo Alto, CA: Learning Policy Institute, 2018.

Deming, W. Edwards. Retrieved from https://www.goodreads.com/author/quotes/310261.W_Edwards_Deming.

Dufour, Richard, Rebecca Dufour, Robert Eaker, and Thomas Many. *Learning by Doing: A Handbook for Professional Learning Communities at Work.* Bloomington, IN: National Education Service, 2006.

Fullan, Michael. *The Change Leader*, 2002. Retrieved from https://www.slideshare.net/ohedconnectforsuccess/6-14-connect-for-success-leadership-presentation.

Fullan, Michael, and Joanne Quinn. "Coherence Making: How Leaders Cultivate the Pathway for School and System Change with a Shared Process." *School Administrator* June 2016: 30–34.

Gordon, Jon. September 25, 2017. Email interview.

Gordon, Jon. July 28, 2016. Personal interview.

Henderson, Anne, Vivian Johnson, Karen Mapp, and Don Davies. *Beyond the Bake Sale: The Essential Guide to Family School Partnerships.* USA: The New Press, WW Norton. Villanova University, 2007.

Hogan, Chris. July 15, 2019. Personal interview.

Keller, Helen Quotes. BrainyQuote.com, BrainyMedia Inc, 2020. https://www.brainyquote.com/quotes/helen_keller_382259, accessed July 8, 2020.

Khalifa, Muhammad A., Mark Anthony Gooden, and James Earl Davis. "Culturally Responsive School Leadership: A Synthesis of the Literature." *Review of Educational Research* 86, no. 4 (2016): 1272–1311.

Klem, Adena M., and Connell, James P. "Relationships Matter: Linking Teacher Support to Student Engagement and Achievement." *Journal of School Health* 74, no. 7 (2004): 262–273.

Koyenikan, Idowu Quote. "Peter Economy. 17 Really Inspiring Quotes on the Tremendous Power of Teamwork." Inc.com. Retrieved on July 8, 2020 from https://www.inc.com/peter-economy/17-inspiring-quotes-on-remarkable-power-of-teamwork.html.

Louis, Karen, Keith Leithwood, Kyla Wahlstrom, and Steven Anderson. *Learning From Leadership: Investigating the Links to Student Learning.* New York: The Wallace Foundation, 2010.

National Association of Elementary School Principals. "The Principal's Guide to Building Culturally Responsive Schools." 2018. Retrieved from https://www.naesp.org/principal-s-guide-building-culturally-responsive-schools.

National Association of Secondary School Principals. "Position Statement: Culturally Responsive Schools." 2019. Retrieved from https://www.nassp.org/policy-advocacy-center/nassp-position-statements/culturally-responsive-schools/.

National Education Association. "Preparing 21st Century Students for a Global Society: An Educator's Guide to the "Four Cs."" n.d. Retrieved from http://www.nea.org/assets/docs/A-Guide-to-Four-Cs.pdf.

National Policy Board for Educational Administration. *Professional Standards for Educational Leaders.* Reston, VA, 2015.

Roosevelt, Theodore. "Theodore Roosevelt Quotes." BrainyQuote.com, BrainyMedia Inc, 2020. Retrieved July 8, 2020 from https://www.brainyquote.com/quotes/theodore_roosevelt_140484.

Spears, Larry C. "Character and Servant Leadership: Ten Characteristics of Effective, Caring Leaders." *The Journal of Virtues & Leadership* 1 (2010): 5–30.

The National Mentoring Partnership. 2016. Retrieved from https://www.mentoring.org/new-site/wp-content/uploads/2016/03/Success-Mentors-School-Checklist.FINAL_.pdf.

Tucker, Pamela, and James H. Stronge. "Linking Teacher Evaluation and Student Learning." ASCD, 2005.

U.S. Department of Education. *Civil Rights Data Collection (CRDC)*. 2020. Retrieved from https://www2.ed.gov/about/offices/list/ocr/data.html.

U.S. Department of Education. *Laws & Guidance School Climate and Discipline: Know the Data*. 2020. Retrieved from https://www2.ed.gov/policy/gen/guid/school-discipline/data.html.

Whitaker, Todd. *What Great Teachers Do Differently: Seventeen Things That Matter Most*. Larchmont, New York: Eye on Education, 2012.

Zardoya, Irma. "What School Leaders Must Learn about Equity: ESSA Offers an Opportunity to Improve Cultural Competence." *Education Week*. February 13, 2017.

/

Index

About the Contributors

Dr. James G. Allen is an associate professor in educational leadership in the College of Education at Northern Kentucky University and teaches courses within the *Teacher as Leader* (MAEd), *Education Specialist* (EdS), and *Educational Leadership* (EdD) programs. Additionally, he serves as the director for the EdD program in educational leadership and most recently served as the interim dean for the College of Education. Prior to his arrival at NKU, he served as assistant professor, associate professor, chair, and assistant dean within the School of Education at Antioch University in Yellow Springs, Ohio. Jim started his career in PK-12 education where he served as an elementary teacher, assistant principal, and acting principal. Dr. Allen earned a BS in elementary education, MEd in educational administration, and EdD in urban educational leadership from the University of Cincinnati.

Dr. Janet L. Applin is an associate professor in Educational Administration, Leadership & Research at Western Kentucky University where she has been a faculty member for sixteen years. From 2012 to 2016, she was associate dean for Academic Programs in the College of Education and Behavioral Sciences. Prior to joining WKU, Janet was a public school special education teacher for fifteen years at all levels. Janet completed her PhD and MEd at Vanderbilt University and her undergraduate studies at Murray State University in Special Education. Her research interests lie in Special Education Administration and Leadership, Curriculum Development, and Advocacy and Equity issues for all children.

Dr. Ginger Blackwell is a clinical associate professor in Northern Kentucky University's College of Education. Prior to coming to NKU, Dr. Blackwell worked for twenty-seven years in Kentucky public schools where she served in a variety of roles, including high school English teacher, elementary and middle grades library media specialist, high school assistant principal, high school principal, and assistant superintendent for teaching and learning.

Dr. Blackwell has been at NKU since 2017 and teaches courses across multiple programs in the College of Education, including the teacher education program, the principal preparation program, and the EdD. program. In addition to her role as a professor, she also serves as the director for educational placements and internships.

Dr. Ann H. Burns, EdD, is an associate professor of educational leadership in the College of Education at Eastern Kentucky University. She is a former classroom teacher, school, district, and Kentucky Department of Education administrator with more than thirty years of experience in leading school improvement, developing systems for continuous improvement, and coaching for school success.

Dr. Greg Goins is a visiting professor at Georgetown College (KY) where he also serves as the director of the Educational Leadership Program. Previously, Dr. Goins served twenty-three years as a P-12 educator in Illinois that included fifteen years as a school district superintendent. Dr. Goins is the founder and host of the nationally acclaimed Reimagine Schools Podcast that is part of the Education Podcast Network and is a popular speaker on education reform and digital leadership. As a former journalism major, Dr. Goins spends his free time covering University of Kentucky basketball and football as a contributing writer and photographer for A Sea of Blue.

Dr. Michael Kessinger is an associate professor of Education Leadership at Morehead State University, College of Education in the Foundational and Graduate Studies department. He received his Doctor of Education in Administration and Supervision from the University of Kentucky, both Education Specialist in Curriculum and Instruction and Master in Secondary Education degrees from Morehead State University, and his undergraduate degree in mathematics and psychology from the University of Wisconsin—Eau Claire.

His background includes thirty-eight years with the Martin County (Kentucky) School System where he served as high school mathematics and computer science teacher, and high school assistant principal. Upon moving to the central office, his duties included coordinating services in gifted education, assessment, professional learning, and technology. He served as director of federal program, finance officer, and assistant superintendent. During that same time, he taught for several community colleges and four-year universities in the areas of mathematics, computer science, educational research, school law, foundations of education, psychology, and education leadership. His research interests and publications include gifted education, professional development, education technology, and school leadership.

Stacy Noah is a Principal Partnership Project (P3) Leadership Specialist in the Kentucky Department of Education's (KDE) Office of Educator Licensure and Effectiveness. She works closely with principals and assistant principals to provide Initial Certified Evaluation Training and long-term professional support. Serving the Commonwealth as a KDE employee since 2012, she has been an active facilitator, professional development lead, and coach for schools and districts across the state in best practice implementation of Kentucky's Growth and Effectiveness System.

Before transitioning to KDE, Noah accrued nearly twenty years of service in Kentucky public schools where she expanded her professional skill set by serving as a high school English teacher, District Achievement Gap Coordinator, high school assistant principal, and middle/high school principal. She holds a Library Media Specialist degree as well as Superintendent Certification.

Dr. Deborah Powers is a thirty-six-year educator currently serving as an assistant clinical professor and the Educational Administration and Leadership program director in the College of Education and Human Development at the University of Louisville. Dr. Powers retired from public school education in May 2018 and joined the faculty at the University of Louisville later that year. She had previously been employed at the University of Louisville from 2008 to 2012 and served as the founding director of the Kentucky Principals Academy (KPA) during that time.

Dr. Powers was a middle school classroom teacher for seventeen years prior to moving into school administration. She has served in both public and private schools, and two different tenures with the Kentucky Department of Education in addition to her time at the University of Louisville. Dr. Powers holds her BA and her MA from the University of Kentucky and her EdD from the University of Louisville.

Dr. Eve Proffitt is currently the Project Specialist, Office of Educator Licensure and Effectiveness, Kentucky Department of Education. Dr. Proffitt has worked in education for forty-eight years. She has been the director of P20 Lab and clinical professor of Educational Leadership at the University of Kentucky, dean of Education and professor of Graduate Education at Georgetown College, special education director and director of data with the Kentucky School Boards Association, associate superintendent of Special Pupil Service, federal projects coordinator, principal, elementary and special education teacher with the Fayette County School District. She served as International President of Phi Delta Kappa.

Dr. Proffitt received her BA and MA from Eastern Kentucky University and her EdS and EdD from the University of Kentucky. She is a national curriculum auditor as well as curriculum trainer with CMSi and Phi Delta Kappa. She has conducted and/or participated in over seventy-five curriculum audits since 1978.

Jenny Ray is currently leadership specialist coordinator leading the Principal Partnership Project (P3) with the Kentucky Department of Education. Previously she served as a professional growth and effectiveness statewide consultant, a mathematics specialist and consultant, a high school principal, a high school math teacher and department chairperson, and a high school math teacher.

Ms. Ray received her Bachelor of Science in mathematics and Master's Degree in Education from Georgetown College. She holds a Rank I in Instructional Leadership and Principalship from Northern Kentucky University. She completed her Superintendent Preparation Program from Northern Kentucky University.

Dr. Stephanie Sullivan has been an educator for thirty years, formerly serving in the K-12 setting as a teacher, counselor, and administrator. As principal, she led her school to achieve National Blue-Ribbon School status, and she was named 2008 Administrator of the Year by the National Association of Elementary School Principals. Currently, she is an assistant professor at Murray State University and coordinator of the Education Administration program. She collaborates with districts in the region to build leadership capacity through the Institute for School Leadership Development.

Dr. Franklin B. Thomas is currently an assistant professor of education at Campbellsville University in Kentucky, where he primarily teaches courses for aspiring principals and action research courses for students seeking their master's degree. He holds a BS in mathematics and an MS in Secondary Education from the University of Kentucky. He also holds a Rank I in Educational Administration and an EdD in Educational Policy Studies from Eastern Kentucky University. He began in public P-12 education in 1989 as a substitute teacher and retired thirty years later as a director of human resources/director of pupil personnel and overseer of a district Save-the-Children Program. In between, he was a high school teacher (and school-based decision-making council member), highly skilled educator at the Kentucky Department of Education, high school assistant principal, middle school principal, curriculum coordinator, instructional supervisor, and district assessment coordinator. He also served one term as president of the Kentucky Association for Assessment Coordinators; was a member of the Kentucky School Curriculum, Assessment, and Accountability Council; is an alumnus of the Kentucky Leadership Academy; and is a member of Phi Beta Kappa.

Dr. Rocky Wallace is an associate professor of Education at Campbellsville University, helping develop CU's graduate education leadership program. He has also served in a similar capacity in helping grow school leader models at Asbury University and Morehead State University, and provides consulting to P-12 schools on integrating the principles of servant leadership into school culture and school improvement.

Rocky is a former school principal of a U.S. Blue-Ribbon School (Catlettsburg Elementary in Catlettsburg, Ky.), served in the Highly Skilled Educator program at the Kentucky Department of Education, and as director of Instructional Support and Adult Education at KEDC (an education cooperative in Ashland, KY).

Rocky earned his doctorate from Regent University in 2007, and since that time has authored or co-authored nine books on servant leadership and school improvement with Rowman & Littlefield.

Dr. Teresa Wallace currently serves as the associate dean of Advanced Programs in the School of Education at the University of the Cumberlands, a private, faith-based institution grounded in Christian principles and leadership through service. Dr. Wallace came to UC in 2015 after spending twenty-five years in public P-12 education. Her P-12 experience includes elementary teacher, principal, district instructional leader, and twelve years as superintendent. Dr. Wallace continues to be involved in P-12 education by serving as a university representative to the regional educational cooperative to which UC belongs, serving on the P-12 Advisory Committee to the UC School of Education, advising administrative program candidates, and teaching courses in the administrative programs.

Dr. Rosemarie (Rosie) Young, EdD, serves as the chair of the EdS and MAED programs at Bellarmine University in Louisville, KY, and the executive director of the Kentucky Association of Elementary School Principals. She worked in the Jefferson County Public Schools for thirty-eight years, twenty-eight years as an elementary school principal. In 2011, she was named Kentucky's National Distinguished Principal for 2012. She holds certification in elementary education 1–8, school guidance counselor, principalship, ECE supervisor, and superintendency. Rosie served on the national committee that developed the National Educational Leadership Preparation (NELP) Standards. She serves as a lead site visitor and team member for the Council for the Accreditation of Educator Preparation (CAEP). She earned her BA from Bellarmine University, her MEd from the University of Louisville, and her EdD from Spalding University.

Made in the USA
Monee, IL
02 September 2022

13081198R00094